REMINISCING IN AFRICA

ALSO BY HAROLD F. MILLER

Encounters in Africa

Reflections in Africa

The Murang'a Murals (editor)

Reminiscing in Africa

Harold F. Miller

NAIROBI

Copyright © Harold F. Miller 2021

ISBN: 978-9966-1988-0-8

The right of Harold F. Miller to be identified as the author of this work has been asserted by him in accordance with the law.

A catalogue record for this book is available from the British Library.

All rights reserved.

The author has checked sources and references for this book, making every effort to ensure the information herein was correct at press time. As such, any errors or omissions are unintended and regretted: the author and publisher do not assume and hereby disclaim any liability to any party for any loss, damage, or disruption caused by errors or omissions, whether such errors or omissions result from negligence, accident, or any other cause.

Published by Manqa Books
www.manqa.net

Cover art: adapted detail of a multi-panel carved mural by Expedito Mwebe Kibbula located in the foyer of the All Africa Conference of Churches headquarters, Nairobi, Kenya
(Photos by E.M./Manqa)
Editing by Keith Miller and Edward Miller
Book design by Edward Miller and Keith Miller

First Edition
10 9 8 7 6 5 4 3 2

For Annetta, Keith, and Edward

To reminisce: to recall past experience with pleasure; to indulge in enjoyable recollection of past events; to recall, to recollect, to reflect on, to call to mind (dictionary)…with a wince, a sigh, and a smile (Harold F. Miller)

> The past is never dead; it is not even past.
> —William Faulkner

> The past is mutable, forever subjected to interpretation—not only by us, but by those whose telling of the past we filter through our own minds.
> —Jean-Paul Sartre

Contents

Introduction   1

1. A Liberation Century in Africa: Mennonites in Ecumenical Collaboration   7
2. Peacemaking in the Horn of Africa: A Local Initiative   32
3. The "Food Decade" in Africa   36
4. Approaches to Grassroots Development   43
5. Food Politics in Africa   53
6. Appropriate Technology: A Candle in the Dark?   59
7. Reflections on the Rural Development Program of the National Council of Churches of Kenya (1974–1981)   71
8. Darfur Ecumenical Visit   104
9. Development as Exotica   113
10. Ecumenical Dimensions in Africa   119
11. Nyerere's Gospels   138
12. The Quest for an Open Sudan   147
13. An Encounter with *Fan into Flame* by John G. Gatu   153
14. Making Peace with the Future: Perspectives on the Relief-Development Mix   160
15. Testing Perceptions on the Gulf War   167
16. Joint Theological Conference: Observations and Comments   172
17. Publications Supported by MCC   186
18. Discerning the Times: Africa's Quest for a Future   198

About the Author   203

Introduction

ANNETTA, MY AMAZING SPOUSE, and I lived, worked, and for a decade retired in Africa over a period of fifty-three years—from 1965 to 2018. As of this writing we live in Harrisonburg, Virginia. We reminisce, we write, we share as would Rip van Winkle with relatives, friends, strangers, scholars, and purveyors of African lore from far and near.

Various impulses had pushed and pulled us to the African continent. Both of us were born and nurtured within communities of intense Christian faith. Annetta was born to missionary parents in Tanganyika (Tanzania); I was born to Amish parents in Hartville, Ohio. We were constantly kept aware of others, near and far, by means of diverse service programs. Christian motives for engagement in service were emphasized and fused variously with the vagaries of cross-cultural wanderlust, social complexities, and learnings.

We married immediately after graduation from Eastern Mennonite College (now University), and were soon employed as teachers in the nearby Eastern Mennonite High School, she in music and I in history and civics. After three years of teaching high school, Annetta declared, "I want to go home." "Home" for her was Tanzania. In consequence, we applied for teaching positions in East Africa with the Teachers Abroad Program (TAP) sponsored by the Mennonite Central Committee.

Our applications to Mennonite Central Committee were redirected, midstream, to the Eastern Mennonite Board of Missions and a staff position within the Christian Council of Tanzania for myself and engagement in music teaching and research in the fledgling conservatoire of music for Annetta. We arrived in Dar es Salaam, Tanzania, in June 1965.

Prior to the departure for Tanzania, we had nurtured an eagerness to be in Africa to witness the momentous transition period then underway, when African countries under European colonial rule since 1884–85 were being transformed, one by one, into independent nation states. We could not have imagined the intensity of that transition period. Nor could we have appreciated or anticipated the complexity of the corollary process then underway in Africa's missionary-founded churches, where leadership was being transferred from foreign missionaries, mostly from North Atlantic countries, to indigenous African church leaders. The urgent mood of the times was captured by a frequently noted comment from Julius Nyerere, the first president of newly independent Tanganyika: "Everything is priority."

Some weeks after our arrival in Dar es Salaam, Chinese premier Zhou Enlai made a state visit to Tanzania. Cold War sentiments of the day were strong, tweaked by President Nyerere to Tanzania's advantage, much to the annoyance of Western democracies.

A resident corps of Western news reporters was in attendance during a public meet-the-press session with Zhou Enlai. From one reporter came the cheeky question: "What is your opinion of the French Revolution of 1789?" Replied the premier: "It is still a bit too early to make a conclusive comment!"

This exchange was much discussed in both the local Tanzanian and the international press. It was deemed an astute comment on the competing political and ideological options on offer, at the time, from the Marxist "East" and the capitalist "West." More than half a century later, Zhou Enlai's cautious comment still resonates, but now in the context of vicissitudes to be faced and choices to be made by the people living in Africa's fifty-five countries (fifty-four sovereign states).

Context for the essays in this volume is provided by the personalities, discussions, processes, upheavals, events, and resolutions that came to my attention during this intense transition period. Soon after our arrival in Dar es Salaam, the pivotal role of Tanzania, and in particular the role of President Julius Kambarage Nyerere, in the African independence/liberation process became apparent. In 1957, Ghana had become the first sub-Saharan African country to achieve political independence. By the time of our arrival in Tanzania, many African countries had followed the precedent set by Ghana, while countries in southern Africa were variously resisting the continental trend.

South Africa had been governed since the 1600s in a variety of configurations by European immigrants, dominated by people from the Netherlands and Great Britain. Beginning in 1948, the National Party, led by Dutch Afrikaner politicians, had introduced and enforced strict apartheid or segregationist policies to the advantage of its minority European population. Neighboring South West Africa (later Namibia) was being administered by South Africa as a United Nations trust territory. Already since the 1500s, the territories of Mozambique, Angola, Guinea-Bissau, and São Tomé and Príncipe had been deemed integral "departments" (not colonies) of Portugal. Rhodesia (later Zimbabwe) was being governed by a minority European settler community.

In 1963, the heads of newly independent African nation states established the Organization of African Unity (OAU), headquartered in Addis Ababa, Ethiopia. A subcommittee known as the OAU Liberation Committee was established in the same year, with headquarters in Dar es Salaam, where President Nyerere served as chair. It was commissioned to work for political independence and majority rule in the countries of southern Africa. In consequence, representatives of liberation movements from southern African countries established offices in Dar es Salaam, seeking recognition and legitimation from the OAU's liberation committee. President Nyerere also served as chairman of a loosely organized group of so-called frontline states, dedicated as well to political independence and majority rule in the continent's southern reaches. Dar es Salaam exuded an intense vibrancy, focused on the promise of a politically independent African continent.

It was widely understood that majority rule in South Africa would serve as the signature achievement of the continental quest for liberation. Many South African nationalists lived and died during that prolonged struggle. Among those, an articulate activist lawyer by the name of Nelson Mandela eventually focused national, continental, and international attention on South Africa's apartheid regime. Following twenty-seven years of incarceration, Mandela was finally released on February 11, 1990. On April 26, 1994, Nelson Mandela was inaugurated as South Africa's first president from the majority populace. Independent Africa, together with governments and peoples around the world, exhaled in solidarity. With continental political independence achieved, other unfinished agenda called for attention.

During the month of April 1994, the politically independent country of Rwanda collapsed under the weight of an interethnic genocide, carried out in a hand-to-hand killing spree, leaving nearly a million people dead. Sudan, Africa's largest country, was fraught by the contentious politics of ethnicity, religion, and ideology. It had declared independence from Anglo-Egyptian rule in 1956. Soon thereafter, civil war broke out between the "Arab" Muslim government and "black African," nominally Christian rebels from southern Sudan. Following seventeen years of civil strife, the Addis Ababa Peace Agreement of 1972 was negotiated and accepted. Ten years later, another round of north–south tensions embroiled Sudan. After years of protracted negotiations, it was finally agreed that South Sudan be established as an independent country on July 9, 2011. As of this writing, it is recognized as Africa's and the world's youngest nation state. This was an achievement subsequently plagued by further internecine armed conflict, resulting in the exit from South Sudan of tens of thousands of refugees to neighboring countries, and in starvation and economic collapse within the newly established country. Meanwhile, Sudan, the immediate neighbor to the north, was wracked by massive public unrest, with protesters insisting on the installation of a civilian government to replace the thirty-year military rule of Omar al-Bashir. Subsequent negotiations have resulted in a shaky but workable coalition government, moving slowly toward a future that, as of this writing, is still being defined.

In the context of global political, economic, and ideological considerations, the influence of erstwhile European colonial powers in Africa is waning, while China, Russia, India, and Turkey are becoming conspicuous actors. Ironically, African countries rank among the poorest, and at the same time feature some of the highest economic growth rates in the world. These realities are seasoned, on the one hand, by would-be emigrants, desperate

Africans seeking asylum and economic opportunity in Europe; and on the other by a significant African diaspora in various Western countries. African immigrants to the United States since the independence decades of the 1960s and '70s are better educated than the average American. In Kenya, the Central Bank reports that remittances from Kenyans living abroad have reached $249 million per month, representing one of the largest sources of foreign currency available to the country. Meanwhile, China has become a dominant economic trading partner and a premier source of funds for infrastructure expansion in Africa.

With regard to modern religious praxis, Africa occupies center stage. As of this writing, approximately 50 percent of African peoples (500 million) are adherents of Islam and approximately 50 percent are adherents of some form of Christianity. Africa has become a global center of Christianity, featuring two of the world's ancient churches—the Egyptian Orthodox Church and the Orthodox Tewahedo Church of Ethiopia—in addition to a complex mixture of Western missionary-initiated churches, amid a plethora of "African Instituted Churches" (AICs). Following the extensive leadership shift from missionaries to African Christians and the accompanying identity quest, African Christianity is engaged with the indigenization of diverse expressions of Pentecostalism.

At the continental level, two African organizations—the African Union (a political/economic entity headquartered in Addis Ababa, Ethiopia) and the All Africa Conference of Churches (a Protestant/ecumenical entity headquartered in Nairobi, Kenya)—have engaged with each other since their common 1963 birth year on matters of mutual interest. With a view toward the centenary year of 2063, the two organizations are collaborating in a common quest to articulate continental moral and ethical norms. In the wake of centuries of tumultuous exogenous exploitation, the accompanying slave trade, and colonial rule, the peoples of Africa are working toward what they hope will be a more promising future.

Words are not adequate to express my gratitude for the privilege of witnessing more than a half century of Africa's pivotal transition period. This collection of musings (the third volume in a series) does not claim to be a definitive analysis of Africa. At best, it offers subjective glimpses into a variety of spaces, issues, times, places, and personal engagements. These are intended neither as introductory nor conclusive observations on the African peoples or the African continent. In this accumulated form, they provide recourse to personal memories. If at the general readership level they stimulate interest in more definitive, more authoritative commentary on Africa, they will have served a modest purpose.

1
A Liberation Century in Africa: Mennonites in Ecumenical Collaboration

Introduction

This survey examines Mennonite collaboration with African ecumenical communities from the early 1960s to the present, in the context of a continental quest for liberation from imperial and minority rule. During this period, the lines delineating the grand Protestant ecumenical project—heir to the missionary initiative from North Atlantic countries—and the grand political project became blurred by the relentless dynamics of history.

African liberation took many forms. In South Africa, resistance leaders deployed both biblical and secular pacifist language. Leaders of the Mau Mau movement in Kenya deployed the language of indigenous religious ideology. Others deployed a modern, secular language. During the height of the Cold War, armed resistance to colonial regimes was supported by Marxist ideology and Marxist language. During the 1960s and '70s, prominent leaders in the African ecumenical movement coined strident theo-biblical language in support of the continent's liberation.

The African liberation project can be understood variously as rebellion against colonial domination, as a refutation of racism, as indigenous religious assertion, as a continental resistance dynamic, as an affirmation of all things African—including the diverse cultures of the diaspora, as a secular voice, as interfaith collaboration, as ecumenical solidarity, and as a quest to join the modern world on African terms. Mennonites supported the African liberation project with the assets at hand, including skilled personnel, Christian solidarity and community, biblical pacifist reflection, and material aid. Precise alignment of the Mennonite response language with African liberation project language was probably never undertaken. Both were in formation; both deployed language deemed appropriate to the relational and activist service expectations of the day.

Political Backdrop

In 1900, the African continent was under the control of European powers, Liberia and Ethiopia the only exceptions. For centuries prior to 1900, Africa had served as a free-for-all arena in the service of European imperial rapacity and Arab trading networks. Both Europeans and Arabs were in pursuit of slaves and ivory, essential trading "commodities" of the day. Then, during the Berlin Conference of 1884-85, the European powers, including Britain, Germany, Portugal, Belgium, Italy, Spain, and France, agreed to delimit and parcel out the continent among themselves. The exercise bestowed a modicum of perverse order onto an otherwise obscene "scramble for Africa." It was an "order" that over the next century would be challenged and altered by a range of dynamics, including the initiatives by members of the African diaspora and African nationalists on the continent, and later by Africa's fledgling Christian ecumenical movement. If those initiatives were slow to birth and slow to gain momentum, by the end of the century their composite effect would prove remarkable.

Resistance from the African diaspora to European colonial rule was reflected in two streams of action. The first was the secular, intellectual, and revolutionary Pan-Africanist movement with Afro-Caribbean roots. The second was "Ethiopianism," informed by the religious, prophetic tradition, a dynamic inspired by scripture ("Princes shall come out of Egypt; Ethiopia shall soon stretch out her hands unto God"—Psalm 68:31) and rooted in the "exhortations of conspiratorial slave preachers." In North America, Ethiopianism was manifest among African Americans as a back-to-Africa movement, reaching a crescendo from 1870 to 1920. On the African continent, Ethiopianism was manifest as a wariness or chafing among African Christians with regard to the tutelage of missionary leadership. In the United States, the movement produced strong leadership personalities such as Marcus Garvey, with roots in Jamaica, who himself never visited Africa but made a career of championing the cause of Mother Africa. Ethiopianism was given eloquent intellectual expression by transition personalities such as Edward Wilmot Blyden from the Caribbean, who spent a lifetime in Liberia as a missionary educator, civic leader, and advocate for Africa (Blyden 1887). With the establishment of Liberia (1847) and Sierra Leone (1808) by returning formerly enslaved African Americans, the political and religious vision of the "Ethiopian" movement had been realized, if only in an interim symbolic fashion (Kalu, 264–74). It was the unflagging secular Pan-Africanists who persevered in the political quest for independence throughout the African continent.

Prominent in the Pan-Africanist Movement were personalities such as Sylvester Williams, George Padmore, George Thomas (later known as Ras Makonnen), C. L. R. James, and W. E. B. Du Bois, hailing from the Caribbean and Guyana. These revolutionary intellectuals of African descent made their way toward Africa via the North American and European metropoles, working in diverse modes for changes in the fortunes of the African continent. Along the way, they sought out and identified with scattered students and young nationalists from Africa who were also struggling for change. Their initiatives eventually coalesced into a coordinated resistance to European imperial control of Africa.

From 1900 to 1945, these and other Pan-Africanists staged a series of seminal congresses, among which the Fifth Pan-African Congress, convened in Manchester, UK, was of pivotal importance. Participants included personalities from the diaspora, but also rising African nationalist stars such as Jomo Kenyatta of Kenya and Kwame Nkrumah of Ghana. After achieving independence in 1957, the first in sub-Saharan Africa, Ghana quickly emerged as a major reference point for follow-up to the previously convened Pan-Africanist Congresses. The resistance dynamics of Pan-Africanism and African nationalism drew heavily on secular ideologies of the day, including revolutionary Marxist and many shades of socialist ideologies. Kwame Nkrumah, articulate African nationalist and independent Ghana's first president, summed up the mood of the day:

"Seek ye first the political kingdom and all else shall be added unto you" (Hastings 1979, 86).

By the end of the 1960s, a great swath of African colonies had attained political independence, followed in the mid-1970s by the Portuguese territories of Mozambique, Angola, Guinea-Bissau, Cape Verde, and São Tomé and Príncipe. Later, the minority "white" governments in Southern Africa succumbed to the continental independence dynamic: Zimbabwe, formerly Rhodesia, in 1980; Namibia, formerly South West Africa, in 1990; and, most dramatically, South Africa in 1994. Having been ignited by a restless and creative African diaspora and joined by an array of African nationalist luminaries, the independence momentum swept across the continent, reflecting a shift in the political "tectonic plates" of global politics. These changes had been ignited in part by Africans who fought in World War II on behalf of the colonial metropoles, defending the colonial enterprise. Collectively, this exposure catapulted the African awareness of cultural identity and political aspirations to unprecedented levels of intensity. Additional momentum was generated by and reflected in the collapse in the early 1990s of the global East–West divide, long sustained by the Cold War.

Ecclesial Backdrop

If the series of Pan-African Congresses represented African political resistance to global colonial rule, the 1910 Edinburgh Mission Conference (a precursor to the subsequent formation of the World Council of Churches) served as an important punctuation point in the global missionary undertaking. Edinburgh marked the end of a remarkable missionary century, facilitated in significant measure by the Pax Britannia, which had provided Western missionary access to countries around the world under colonial tutelage. Attended by participants from young churches across the globe, Edinburgh was an expression of church on a global scale. But there was no official African presence at the conference, even though the African continent had more than 8 million Christians at the time. In Edinburgh, they were represented only indirectly by several Western missionaries.

Having been convened as a recognition of more than one hundred years of Christian mission in other parts of the world, conference participants in Edinburgh opined that the Christian Gospel was unlikely to be readily accepted in Africa because of pervasive indigenous religious belief and praxis. It was the primal religions of Africa, termed "animism," that without doubt caused the most concern (Bediako 1995, 192–3). Eighty-eight years later, it was reported during the World Council of Churches' Eighth General Assembly in Harare, Zimbabwe, that "in Africa and Asia, as well as among the indigenous peoples [elsewhere], Christians are discovering their Christian faith within their own cultures" (WCC report, 1999, 16).

Moreover, according to the widely quoted ecclesial statistician David Barrett, by the year 2000, Africa was estimated to be 48 percent Christian and 41 percent Muslim, with responses to these two missionary religions assumed to have been accomplished at the expense of a corresponding decline in adherence to indigenous African Religion (Barrett 1982, 782 and 789). Less than a century after the Edinburgh Conference, Christianity in Africa had blossomed from negligible numbers to become the numerical center of world Christianity. In the history of Christianity's spread around the world, such rapid growth is unprecedented.

When the wave of political independence swept across Africa in the 1960s, its effects were felt both within the political establishment and within the mainline Protestant, mission-founded churches. African politicians replaced colonial governors and African civil servants replaced the colonial civil servants. Similarly, within Protestant mission communities, missionary leaders were replaced by African church leaders. In the pre-independence period, nascent, mostly Protestant ecumenism had taken the form of National Missionary Fellowships, institutional structures established for purposes of coordinating common efforts in health, education, and Bible translation and distribution work. Among the many changes effected after the independence-induced leadership transfer was the transformation of Missionary Fellowships into National Councils of Churches. Church-related ministries in health and education typically devolved to the care of specialized, self-administering agencies, leaving National Councils of Churches free to address the more immediate issues generated by the dynamics of political and ecclesial independence.

Politico-Ecclesial Project

Like the new corps of African politicians, African church leaders of the day were charged with nationalist independence fervor. Both assumed that the mandate of the Christian church intersected in many ways with the mandate of the new African-led independent governments. Indeed, personal links between leaders of the ecclesial and state structures were close, if only because many church leaders and political leaders had been classmates in missionary-sponsored schools, nurtured by common African visions. But theological articulation of how separate or together church and state were was not so clear, according to John Mbiti, a prominent Kenyan theologian (Chepkwony, 25). To this day, the quest for theological clarity in this regard continues. If there is a discernible pattern or emphasis in the continuing inquiry, current church-state theologies seem to be informed more by the exigencies of genocide, war, displacement, and peace treaties than by an overarching theological framework guiding church-state relationships in the longer term.

In 1963, during the height of the early independence period, these two streams—the political and the ecclesial—undertook similar initiatives at the continental level. Senior African church leaders launched the All Africa Conference of Churches (AACC), an ecumenical organization with a continental reach but with a consultative (conferring) rather than a legislative (conciliar) mandate, featuring an eventual membership of 170 mostly mainline Protestant churches, including several so-called independent African churches in addition to 32 affiliated National Councils of Churches. Several months later, African heads of independent states initiated and launched the Organization of African Unity (OAU), a continental political entity focused on fostering political independence for the southern African countries still saddled with minority or some form of colonial rule. In this context, the OAU mandated the formation of the famous OAU Liberation Committee, subsequently chaired and hosted by Tanzania. The OAU was reconfigured in 2002 with the formation of the African Union (AU).

International and continental African attention was focused during the 1970s on the theater of armed and popular resistance to the remaining colonial or minority "white" regimes in southern Africa. Nelson Mandela, who had already been incarcerated on Robben Island for a decade, was by that time recognized as an international icon of resistance to apartheid rule. Globally, the foundations of the Cold War were cracking, with reverberations coursing through the African continent. Across southern Africa, leaders of liberation wars had victory in their crosshairs. Political change had reached high noon; the African continent was shedding the formal remnants of its colonial shell.

Against this backdrop, the AACC's continental agenda was being formulated. On the one hand, there was the legacy of ecumenical concern for organic church unity, bequeathed by North Atlantic missionary-sending communities divided since Reformation times by the scandal of multiple denominations. On the other hand, mainline churches in Africa could not ignore the ferment of continental political and social realities in the postindependence period. African ecumenical leaders chose to give priority attention to the latter. Thus, during its 1974 General Assembly in Lusaka, Zambia, the AACC gave a nod of theological assent to the armed resistance underway in regions to the south, reflecting the strong liberationist sentiments of the day, but sparking disapproving murmurs in some quarters of the African ecumenical community and beyond—was the spiritual ministry of the church in Africa unduly preoccupied with temporal political concerns? Subsequently, an African academic summarized the dynamics thus: "By seeing Christ at work in the emerging African states, [the African ecumenical church] tied that cosmic figure to African political and economic aspirations, a link that has remained unbroken to this day" (Utuk 1997, 232).

While the advent of political independence in Africa was characterized by much ferment, at the level of the United Nations, the 1960s and '70s were respectively declared the First and Second Development Decades. Those declarations were buttressed by the deliberations of a series of eighteen global UN-sponsored conferences (1972–82), identifying categories and specifying agreed standards by which global human well-being could be ascertained. According to those deliberations, in the new postcolonial world order everyone had the right to the basic amenities necessary to the sustenance and growth of human life. The mood was expansive and optimistic. NGOs that had been created to provide relief to war-ravaged Europe in the 1940s and '50s were now, in the 1960s and '70s, retooling in support of development aspirations in the newly independent countries of Africa.

Enter the Mennonites

Already in the late 1800s, Mennonite and later Brethren in Christ (BIC) mission boards in North America had launched evangelization initiatives in the Congo, Northern Rhodesia (now Zambia), Southern Rhodesia (now Zimbabwe), and Tanganyika (now Tanzania). Compared to mainline Protestant missions and churches, the Mennonites and the BIC were minor actors. But, like virtually all other Protestant churches across the African continent, these mission churches were caught up in the dynamics of independence in the 1960s and the related shift from foreign to African leadership. And as was the case elsewhere, health and education services, formerly offered by the missionary communities, were expected in independent Africa to be made available to the service of the larger public in the context of national social service grids. National missionary fellowships, which had been established to coordinate health and education services, were now transformed into national councils of churches with newly installed African leaders informed by the demands of tumultuous change and the new opportunities offered or implied by self-rule.

Like other North American service or diakonia agencies, MCC was just emerging from post–World War II relief activity in Europe and was now focusing on the African continent. MCC had turned to Africa on an optimistic note, informed by the newly declared UN Development Decades and by the findings of a 1961 UNESCO-sponsored conference in Ethiopia, which identified formal education as a priority for the newly independent countries of Africa. This declared priority was reinforced in UN deliberations and coincided with a decision by MCC's Executive Committee to send a representative to Africa with the mandate to explore the possibilities of support for secondary education in Central Africa.

Thus, in November 1961, Mennonite educator Robert Kreider visited North Rhodesia (Zambia), South Rhodesia (Zimbabwe), and Nyasaland (Malawi), where he spent some days exploring the possibility of placing teachers in secondary schools. His immediate mission and church contact for this purpose was Bishop David Climenhaga of the Brethren in Christ Church with its far-flung mission infrastructure in the region and longstanding official relationships with MCC in North America. Another contact person was David Temple, who was the education secretary for the Northern Rhodesia Christian Council and principal at a teacher training institution. Temple served as a liaison person between the Ministry of Education and the governing councils of the respective secondary schools (*African Christian Pulse* 2005). Why this particular entry point for the MCC initiative? According to Kreider, it was "simply because in Africa the governments of the day, the Councils of Churches and the Brethren in Christ all reported needs in this regard and all indicated a willingness to collaborate with the MCC program immediately" (Kreider 1961).

MCC's ensuing teacher placement initiative in Africa was eventually christened the Teachers Abroad Program (TAP).

East and West Africa

Subsequently, the institutional/relational and teacher-placement model developed by Kreider was extended to other countries in southern Africa, to the three East African countries (Kenya, Tanzania, Uganda), to Congo in the middle of the continent, and to several countries in West Africa. According to a long-term MCC worker in Africa, the TAP model served as the entry point for collaboration between MCC and the national councils of churches in Africa. In part, these links represented relationships of convenience, for in the newly independent countries, the government ministries of education generally relied on the national church councils to provide a liaison function vis-à-vis church- and mission-related schools. But these links were also an expression of MCC's determination from the beginning to relate to a wide range of churches and church institutions in Africa rather than developing its own institutional presence (Lind 1989,

9). In subsequent interactions with councils of churches in a number of southern African countries, MCC's engagement agenda shifted toward a range of issues beyond the initial pattern of placing TAPpers in secondary schools.

Botswana

In Botswana, MCC's support ministries took on a diverse character. Large in landmass, with a semiarid climate and a population at the time well below a million people, featuring only a fledgling modern sector, Botswana was extraordinarily open to the presence and contribution of NGOs such as MCC. Mennonites embraced the country's openness by forging collaboration between MCC and several US-based Mennonite mission boards, resulting in a unique institutional configuration known as Mennonite Ministries. Among the first contacts made by Mennonites were those with the Botswana Council of Churches (BCC). Over subsequent decades, Mennonite agencies seconded more than three hundred people to a variety of positions in Botswana. Some personnel placements followed the TAP model, and some were made in the context of BCC members churches; one Mennonite worker provided financial and secretarial services directly within the BCC office. And for an extended period, Mennonite Ministries served as a permanent member of the BCC executive committee (Rudy 1999, 22). In mid-2005, MCC celebrated forty years of service in Botswana.

If MCC's initial TAP foray into Northern Rhodesia (Zambia) was buoyed by postindependence optimism, the subsequent more generalized attention to southern Africa was informed by "a bewildering complex of currents and crosscurrents which portend[ed] crisis" (Bertsche and Jacobs 1970, 1). South Africa's apartheid system was widely recognized as an affront to the acceptable norms of human community, generally, and to the collective Christian conscience, in particular. Together with this general acknowledgment was the sense among many North American Mennonites in the late 1960s that any involvement within South Africa would be deemed a compromise of Christian conscience. It was considered best to avoid all contact with South Africa and advisable even to refrain from engagement in neighboring countries such as Lesotho, Botswana, and Swaziland. However, a few Mennonite leaders countered with an alternative vision. Following a visit to the region in May 1970, several Mennonite mission administrators began to formulate a Mennonite role in southern Africa: "While the international community holds apartheid in abhorrence, the windows and doors of the Republic [of South Africa] must be forced open from the outside so that the winds of change can blow through. This is Christian responsibility" (Penner 1992).

Southern Africa

Although direct MCC engagement within South Africa was ruled out both by the apartheid government and by general Mennonite sensibilities, work in Swaziland and other so-called frontline states was deemed to provide windows onto the changes that were virtually destined to unfold in South Africa. The first Mennonite country representative in Swaziland spelled out the posture:

> I have never really needed to question the rightness of our being here… I don't see Swaziland as an extremely needy country (by comparison) but there is plenty of scope for Christian concern… It is relevant for us to think of Swaziland in relationship to the whole of Southern Africa… So much is already being done in South Africa by intelligent, sympathetic, enlightened, committed Christians and humanitarians that I find it difficult to believe that we would have anything radically new to bring to the situation. Strengthening what is being done, yes. (Penner 1992)

Swaziland

In the spirit of "strengthening what is already being done," Mennonites in Swaziland forged relationships with a variety of agencies in the country, including the Swaziland Council of Churches (SCC), comprised at the time primarily of member churches with an evangelical character. When a group of Zulu refugees escaped armed conflict in the Natal Province of South Africa in the 1970s, the SCC did not consider response to the refugee needs as part of its mandate. This incident gave rise to the formation of the Council of Swaziland Churches (CSC) with Catholic, Anglican, and Lutheran churches as members, and to a unique ecumenical engagement for Mennonites.

During the formation proceedings of the CSC, a senior Mennonite worker in Swaziland was recruited to serve as its first general secretary. When he protested, "How can I as a foreigner take this position?" he was rebuked by the presiding Roman Catholic bishop: "Did you come to serve the churches in Africa?" "Yes I did." "Then you will do as you are told!" The Mennonite worker accepted the position in a council that would subsequently become affiliated with the World Council of Churches and the All Africa Conference of Churches (Rudy, MA Thesis, 58).

Mozambique

Even as Mennonite workers were being placed in politically independent countries contiguous with South Africa, they were mindful of neighboring Mozambique, functioning till then as an overseas Portuguese territory, but now under the siege of armed freedom fighters. In September 1964, the leading armed liberation movement of Mozambique, FRELIMO, had fired the first bullet in its quest for political independence. At the time, senior officials of the movement were hosted by Tanzania, the country serving as secretary to the OAU's Liberation Committee. During the mid-1960s to the early 1970s, two Mennonite workers were seconded to the Christian Council of Tanzania in Tanzania's capital city, Dar es Salaam. They were assigned to programs supporting Mozambican exiles and refugees in camps hosted by the Tanzanian government, managed by the Lutheran World Federation and funded by the United Nations. Coincidentally, the Mennonite workers in Dar es Salaam had as their nearby neighbors several senior FRELIMO officials, including Edwardo Mondlane, the movement's first president. Even to the casual observer, aspects of Mozambique's liberation war were played out, as it were, on the doorsteps of this Dar es Salaam neighborhood, rendering the armed struggle for change in southern Africa a daily reality (MCC Workbook 1965).

By 1975, Mozambique had achieved its independence from Portugal in the wake of a long and vicious armed independence struggle. Thanks to the strong Marxist ideology nurtured during the FRELIMO's struggle and thanks to the close collaboration between Portugal's Catholic Church and the Portuguese colonial government, churches in Mozambique and the new FRELIMO government of the day were wary of each other. Church–state relationships, already tenuous at independence, became even more fragile when the new FRELIMO government proceeded, soon after assuming authority, to nationalize church-operated schools and hospitals throughout the country. It was in this charged context that MCC dispatched several senior Mennonites to visit newly independent Mozambique.

Meanwhile, the fledgling Christian Council of Mozambique (CCM) was proceeding gingerly, seeking occasion to open dialogue with the government, but avoiding undue confrontation. By means of discreet engagement with certain government leaders, the CCM carefully articulated its right and its perceived duty to participate in the reconstruction of the country. To this end, the CCM was eventually able to mobilize considerable international support. In due time, the CCM emerged as the accepted link between the FRELIMO government and the Protestant churches. Just as a certain uneasiness characterized the church–state relationships within the country, so the Protestant churches in Mozambique were distrustful and fearful of the prospect of overbearing interventions by international church-related service agencies (Rudy 1997, 22).

Fully cognizant of these sensitivities on several fronts, the exploratory visits to Mozambique by senior Mennonites during the mid-1970s were focused on the CCM as the primary point of contact and guided by a carefully articulated relational posture: "Our current stance of supporting [indigenous] church bodies rather than establishing our own in [southern] Africa is a thought out and conscious missiological strategy, based on the assumption that we should strengthen rather than further fragment the Body of Christ and that we can share our understandings of what being a Christian means within other church groups" (Rudy 2000).

These initial Mennonite contacts with the CCM were followed by MCC personnel placement in neighboring Swaziland, with a mandate to provide material aid to Mozambican refugees in Zimbabwe in preparation for repatriation. They also had the mandate to provide material aid to needy areas within Mozambique. Eventually, it was determined that a Mennonite material aid consultant should be placed within the CCM secretariat to facilitate the logistical and administrative procedures related to the material aid being made available through MCC. From these beginnings, the relationships between MCC and CCM went from strength to strength. MCC personnel were subsequently appointed to auxiliary staff positions within the CCM institutional structure and within CCM member churches in various parts of the country.

Transkei

As noted above, MCC's declared strategy was to be present and engaged in countries and territories contiguous with South Africa, given that a presence inside the country was not feasible. In this regard, the Transkei was a special case. The Transkei had been designated by the apartheid regime as an African "homeland" or "Bantustan," and was, according to official South African government policy, politically independent, though that independence was recognized by no other government in the world. This fictional political status imposed on the Transkei was rendered even more fragile when it became evident that the South African regime reserved and exercised the right to intervene in the affairs of the "independent" homeland. MCC's decision in 1978 to be present with the Transkei Council of Churches (TCC) was therefore a decision to be present on a volatile frontline territory.

With origins dating to 1964, the Christian Council of the Transkei took on the status in 1969 of an affiliated regional council of the South African Council of Churches (SACC), at which point it had become designated as the Transkei Council of Churches (TCC). In 1978, MCC seconded staff to the TCC and, in 1981, submitted a request for membership in the TCC. Subsequently, both MCC and Mennonite mission personnel were seconded to staff positions within the TCC offices, to TCC field program positions, and to positions with TCC member churches. Several MCC workers served successively as development consultants to the TCC and, at one point in 1979, an MCC worker kept the central TCC office operational when it was "closed down" during a particularly tense spate of interference by the South African government (MCC Workbook 1978).

Within the TCC, and later in its placement of Mennonite personnel to a variety of positions within South Africa, MCC found itself interacting closely with South African anti-apartheid activists, both within and outside the church context. Even though the South African government kept a watchful eye on MCC activities, placement of MCC personnel within the country became a bit easier as the end of the apartheid period became more and more certain. Among these placements was a dizzying variety of specialized study centers, church-related retreat centers, universities, street children programs, and welfare centers offering peace studies, training in a variety of skills, and overseas sabbaticals for harried anti-apartheid activists, as well as general welfare services. Although MCC had provided a continuous flow of supporting funds to the SACC and maintained close relationships with the organization over an extended period—both before and after Mennonite personnel were placed inside South Africa—the SACC did not serve as MCC's host agency within the country. MCC placed and administered its personnel in South Africa from surrounding countries until the first MCC country representatives were placed in Durban, South Africa, in 1992 (Rudy, 22-35).

Majority Rule in South Africa

Finally, in April 1994, Nelson Mandela was installed as the first African president of South Africa. Before, during, and after his release from twenty-seven years of detention, he had become recognized as an African icon and a global hero. With the independence of South Africa, or more precisely, with the achievement of majority rule in South Africa, the first phase of continental Africa's liberation had been achieved. The "century-long" resistance movement by intellectuals in the diaspora, and by political and church-related activists within South Africa and around the world, had finally come to fruition. Across the African continent and far beyond there was a swell of applause and a huge sense of achievement. One of the world's most intractable open sores had yielded to formidable and sustained pressure (both violent and nonviolent) for change.

"Success has many fathers" goes the saying. Like other agencies involved in southern Africa, MCC was able in a variety of ways to savor the results of solidarity with South Africa's quest for change, appreciating that both the struggle and the successes were defined differently by different actors. For activist resistance politicians, apartheid governance had been viewed as a violation of the rights of the majority; for activist theologians, apartheid had constituted a theological heresy to be denounced, rejected, and replaced with genuinely "good news." MCC had perceived apartheid as a distorted governance system supported by a false theology and false politics requiring radical, but preferably peaceful, change.

Post-Apartheid

When a relatively peaceful transition was in fact realized, few solidarity actors, including MCC personnel, had anticipated that significant numbers of South Africa's church-related anti-apartheid activists would now be joining the newly formed majority government. Initially, the shift had the effect of crippling the SACC and rendering visible an astonishing array of unresolved dynamics. These included issues such as the viability of the prevailing nation-state model in Africa, the relevance of the ongoing discussion regarding the African Renaissance (Hord and Lee 1995), the rights and the functional identities of ethnic and minority groupings, the control and deployment of natural resources, and the vicissitudes of urbanization. From MCC's point of view, these were issues to be addressed in the context of fresh exploration of indigenous understandings, including the more broadly based practices of conflict resolution, restorative justice, reconciliation, and healing.

In an attempt to engage precisely with such an array of issues in the post-apartheid context, MCC seconded a worker couple to Letsema, a program of the Wilgespruit Fellowship Center in Roodepoort, near Johannesburg. From the Wilgespruit base, MCC workers in 2001 established and subsequently supported a program known as the Africa Peace Institute (API), hosted by the Mindolo Ecumenical Foundation, located near Kitwe, Zambia. API enjoyed a collaborative collegial relationship with Eastern Mennonite University in Harrisonburg, Virginia, and from its inception received financial support from MCC. It mounted an annual intensive six-week course in conflict resolution and peace studies from a Christian perspective, catering for students from across Africa who were pursuing academic certificates, professional enrichment, and personal development and growth. Instruction combined theory and practice for conflict resolution through applied study on topics such as peacebuilding, nonviolence, intervention roles, trauma healing, and reconciliation (Stauffer, Carl and Carolyn 2002).

For decades, the continental African anti-apartheid project had provided a point of cohesive solidarity for a disparate range of activists and politicians. Within the precincts of the OAU, for example, Africa's heads of state readily achieved consensus on anti-apartheid statements even as they disagreed vehemently on other issues of continental import. During the very month when South Africa was hailing success, sharp-eyed members of the international press corps, many of them covering the South African events, were also publicizing the onset of the Rwanda genocide, exploding into a prime exhibit of an African and an international tragedy. For anyone who cared to notice, the advent of genocide in an independent, predominantly "Christian" African country signaled the launch, or served as an ominous reminder, of the continent's unfinished business at that tumultuous post-apartheid and postindependence juncture.

Sudan

Beginning already in the 1600s, southern Africa had been variously convulsed by "apartheid" politics, although explicit and unapologetic racist rule was most pronounced from 1948 to 1994, a period when the "white" Nationalist Party held the reins of power. Sudan, Africa's largest country, had an equally tortured history. For centuries, this vast territory had been invaded and plundered by foreign powers. In 1956, the country achieved a form of political independence, but the government of the day was deemed by southern Sudanese to represent a racist "Arab" minority. Nearly a half century of armed rebel activity in the modern era resulted in complex, painstakingly negotiated peace agreements. The provisions of the January 2005 agreements between rebels and the government of Sudan were slowly and painfully implemented.

Relationships between Sudan and other Middle Eastern countries have been diverse and extensive. Five of the ruling pharaohs in Egypt were of Nubian (northern Sudanese) origin. Pyramids, those unique physical structures usually associated with Egypt, are also found in northern Sudan. People from northern Sudan (Nubia) served in the armies of Egypt "from time immemorial," and trade within and beyond the Nile Valley has "always been there." Forty years after Pentecost, a Nubian man became the first African Christian south of Egypt (Acts 8:26-40). Centuries later, Nubia was evangelized jointly by the ancient Church of Constantinople and by the Coptic (Egyptian) Church, giving birth to a Nubian Christian community that flourished for nearly a thousand years (AD 500 to AD 1500).

Following an initial assault in AD 642, Arab Muslims launched a series of incursions into northern Sudan, where they were met and restrained by the armies of Christian Nubian monarchies, whose soldiers were known as the "pupil smiters" due to their uncanny ability to strike enemies in the eyes with arrows! In contrast to other successful conquests, including their conquest of Egypt, the Arab invaders were initially unable to gain control of Nubia. Faced with this, they concluded a *baqt* ("pact") with their Christian Nubian counterparts shortly before the year AD 700. Unprecedented in the annals of Islamic expansion, the pact provided guidelines governing trade between Nubian Christians and Arab Muslims, and restrictions regarding the settlement of Arabs in Nubia. Although Christian Nubia eventually succumbed to Arab suzerainty, the provisions of the pact were adhered to in varying degrees by both parties for nearly six centuries. Extensive commentary and debate among Islamic scholars in successive centuries regarding this pact attest to its unique character (Werner, Anderson, Wheeler, 84-85). Given the continuing modern role of Sudan as bridge between Arab and African, Islam and Christianity, the ancient pact functions as an archetypical reference point.

Modern Christianity in Sudan traces its beginnings to the entry in the mid-1800s of European missionaries. Their endeavors suffered severely under the rule of the "Mahdi" (the Muslim revivalist, the "sent one") in the 1880s, expanded under the joint Anglo-Egyptian rule (1898–1956), and chafed under successive independent Sudanese governments. Even before independence in 1956, aggrieved southern Sudanese triggered an armed rebellion and a seventeen-year civil war, ending in 1972 with the signing of the Addis Ababa Peace Accord. Negotiations leading to this accord had been initiated and brokered by the World Council of Churches and the All Africa Conference of Churches. Following a ten-year period of relatively peaceful respite, civil war resumed and continued for another twenty years. This second phase of the war was resolved with the signing of a peace accord in 2005 between the Arab-dominated government of Sudan and the Sudan Peoples Liberation Movement/Army (SPLM/A), brokered this time by the Inter-Governmental Agency of Development (IGAD).[1]

As in other African countries, missionaries to Sudan were sponsored by a range of confessional traditions. And, like elsewhere, they quickly found it necessary to collaborate on common efforts in the categories of health, education, and Bible translation; by the mid-1960s, this collaboration took the form of the Sudan Missionary Fellowship. In the late 1960s, the beginnings of the Sudan Council of Churches (SCC) were taking institutional form. Following the 1972 Addis Ababa Peace Accord, the SCC was rendered a more formal institution and equipped by the global ecumenical community to undertake relief and rehabilitation activity, focused on war-ravaged southern Sudan. Between 1972 and 2005, Sudan became the focus of remarkable ecumenical endeavor. MCC's engagement with and support for the Sudanese churches coincides with this period.

Beginning in 1972, MCC seconded personnel to the SCC's Commission for Relief and Rehabilitation, headquartered in Khartoum, and later seconded personnel to a variety of field positions in both northern and southern Sudan. During the turbulent second phase of the civil war (1983–2005), MCC maintained its regional Sudan office in Nairobi,

---

[1] IGAD is a regional (Horn of Africa) inter-governmental agency established by the Governments of Kenya, Uganda, Sudan, Djibouti, Ethiopia, and Somalia. Originally formed in the early 1990s to combat regional locust plagues, it was subsequently mandated and equipped to be engaged with conflict resolution and mediation in Horn of Africa countries.

enabling access to both rebel- and government-held areas. From that base, MCC participated in the early 1980s with the establishment of the Nairobi-based New Sudan Council of Churches (NSCC). Thanks to the intensity of the prevailing civil war in Sudan, the SCC was mandated by the member churches to be present to the government-held areas and the NSCC to rebel-held areas. Another MCC window onto Sudan became possible through collaboration with the AACC. From 1989 to 1999, MCC seconded a staff person to the International Affairs Desk of the AACC who was mandated, among other briefs, to accompany the ecumenical and political vagaries of Sudan.

MCC personnel have continued to participate in the respective ecumenical deliberations, such as annual general assemblies, partner roundtable meetings, and field programs of both SCC and NSCC. Both councils—two expressions of a single ecumenical reality—enjoyed the full participation of Sudanese Catholic and Protestant member churches. At national and regional levels, MCC personnel were active in both the Ecumenical Support Program for Sudan, a solidarity initiative undertaken by the National Council of Churches of Kenya (NCCK), and in the AACC's Sudan Working Group, providing "second-track" diplomatic support for the official Sudan peace process. At the global level, MCC personnel participated in the Sudan Ecumenical Forum, which brought together support agencies from North Atlantic countries and representatives from churches and Christian Councils in Africa.

Throughout the period, peace talks between the government of Sudan and the rebel SPLM were underway, sponsored by IGAD. Churches in Sudan, supported by the whole of the aforementioned ecumenical apparatus, were relentless in their pursuit of peace within the South. Churches and ecumenical partners also maintained close vigilance on the stuttering official peace talks, cajoling, commenting, and advising. When a comprehensive peace agreement between the SPLM and the government of Sudan was finally signed on January 9, 2005, there was a huge sigh of relief and a vast sense of accomplishment across eastern Africa. Within six months after the signing, Col. John Garang, the charismatic leader and negotiator of the SPLM, died in a helicopter crash. An already complex political drama was rendered even more complex.

Paralleling the experience in South Africa after apartheid, senior staff from the respective Christian Councils of Sudan were drawn, after the peace agreement of 2005, into the employ of Sudan's government of national unity. The response of the larger ecumenical community to this development varied. Some held the view that churches should have retained a discrete vigilant posture, separate from government, monitoring the implementation of the peace and sustaining a clear vision for a peaceful future in Sudan. Others perceived the absorption of Christian Council staff into government positions as a vindication of the churches' sustained advocacy for peace over the decades. Did a fragile north-south peace agreement in the Sudan portend a stability pattern for the whole country, or indeed for the continent? By signing a comprehensive agreement with its southern rebels, had the Sudan government finally accepted the contiguity of its African character geographically, politically, culturally, and economically? Did Sudan's ancient Arab-Nubian pact suggest some mega-reference point for national and continental integration? On these and many other questions, the jury's sentiments remained inconclusive.

How can the support of Africa's liberation project and the accompanying development project by the ecumenical movement over the past half century be most helpfully characterized? And how can MCC's eclectic accompaniment of that process be most helpfully characterized?

An African proverb offers some clues: "The whole body bends to remove the thorn from the toe." To the concerned persons of the African diaspora and their African nationalist cohorts, the seminal thorn in the African body politic was the issue of foreign or colonial rule, which had blanketed the continent since the Berlin Conference of 1884–85. In reaction, the whole continent, deploying all available means, was destined for more than a century to "bend" in concerted effort to remove that thorn. Formal education, supported by missionaries and recognized by the variety of colonial governments, raised public awareness in favor of continental liberation. In this context, MCC "bent" very substantial resources of personnel and finance in support of formal education as encouragement and support to newly independent African countries but fully cognizant of the charged southern Africa context.

Concluding Queries

Tragically, the shift from colonial to indigenous rule eventually included the widespread deployment of armed resistance. The most obvious results took the form of independent African governments, replacing colonial rule. But those results were achieved at the cost of enormous suffering and dislocation. Might the same results have been achieved by nonviolent means? Early leaders of South Africa's African National Congress, now the ruling political party, believed so. Throughout the century, leaders of Christian churches in Africa yearned for liberation, but were conflicted theologically and personally by the seeming inevitability of armed resistance.

In what measure was the violence of slavery and the anticolonial armed resistance redeemed at the end of the century by the dynamics of "peaceful" negotiation and expressions of forgiveness in post-apartheid South Africa? Embedded in that question were propositions that have engaged sociopolitical scientists and Christian theologians in deep, unresolved discussion over a period of decades. Did Archbishop Desmond Tutu, a designated continental ecumenical spokesperson and subsequently a Nobel Peace Prize laureate, bespeak an African theological and cultural ethic when he extended the hand of forgiveness to leaders of the Dutch Reformed Churches, long the exponents of an apartheid theology in support of apartheid politics? Was the extended forgiveness too facile, too easily absolving perpetrators of a heinous ideology? Did he, in chairing South Africa's now famous Truth and Reconciliation Commission (TRC), embody and enact healing for a tortured continent? Did he, in authoring *No Future without Forgiveness*, point the African continent toward a viable peaceful future?

Some of Africa's most ardent advocates remain unsated by the proffered forgiveness. MCC, together with many other actors, is left to ponder the meaning of the African century just past, savoring the reality and the challenge of having served in contested "forgiven space" on a continent still on a quest for its better self.

—*Nairobi, Kenya, December 2005*

Sources

Barrett, David B. *World Christian Encyclopedia: A Comparative Survey of Churches and Religions in the Modern World, AD 1900–2000*. 1982. Oxford University Press. Oxford/New York.

Bediako, Kwame. *Christianity in Africa: The Renewal of a Non-Western Religion*. 1995. Orbis Books. Maryknoll, New York.

Bertsche, Jim and Don Jacobs. "Southern Africa Study." May, 1970.

Blyden, Edward Wilmot. *Christianity, Islam and the Negro Race*. 1887. Whittigham Press. London.

Chepkwony, Agnes. *The Role of Non-Governmental Organizations in Development: A Study of the National Christian Council of Kenya 1963–1978*. 1987. Uppsala University. Uppsala, Sweden.

Hastings, Adrian. *A History of African Christianity 1950–1975*. 1979. Cambridge University Press. Cambridge, London, New York.

Hord, Fred Lee and Jonathan Scott Lee. *I Am Because We Are: Readings in Black Philosophy*. 1995. The University of Massachusetts Press. Amherst, Mass.

Kalu, Ogbu U. *African Christianity: An African Story*. 2005. Department of Church History. University of Pretoria. Pretoria, South Africa.

Kreider, Robert. "Letter to Bishop David Climenhaga." November 17, 1961. (Written from Meikles Hotel, Salisbury, Southern Rhodesia.)

Lind, Tim. *MCC Africa Program: Historical Background*. MCC Occasional Paper No. 10. August 1989. Mennonite Central Committee.

Makonnen, Ras. *Pan-Africanism From Within*. (As recorded and edited by Kenneth King.) 1973. Oxford University Press. Nairobi, London, New York.

Mennonite Central Committee. *MCC Workbooks*. 1964 to 2002.

Penner, Peter and Leona. "Southern Africa History Project Proposal." Prepared for discussion at the October 1992 Southern Africa Coordinating Group [MCC representatives' meeting].

Rudy, Jonathan. *Mennonite Committee Zambia: 35 Years—1962–1997*. February 1988. Mennonite Central Committee.

_____. *A Brief History of Mennonites in Swaziland: The First 25 Years*. July 1996. Mennonite Central Committee.

_____. *A Brief History of Mennonite Central Committee in Lesotho*. September 1996. For Mennonite Ministries in Lesotho and Southern Africa Coordinating Group.

_____. *History of Mennonites in Mozambique* (including MCC involvement in Malawi post–1981 program closure). April 1997. Mennonite Central Committee.

_____. *Mennonite Central Committee/Mennonite Ministries–Botswana.* April 1999. Mennonite Central Committee.

_____. *Anabaptists and AICs: A Unique Paradigm for Mission in Southern Africa.* May 2001. A thesis submitted to Eastern Mennonite Seminary in partial fulfilment of the requirements for a Degree of Master of Arts in Religion.

_____. "Abstracts regarding African Christian Councils from MCC service histories." January 27, 2000. In personal communication.

Stauffer, Carl. "Nurturing the Tree of Peace." January–March 2002. *MCC Peace Office Newsletter.*

_____. *The Africa Peace-Building Institute (API) – Zambia: Case Study* (undated brochure).

Tutu, Desmond Mpilo. *No Future Without Forgiveness.* 1999. Random House. London.

Utuk, Efion. *Visions of Authenticity: The Assemblies of the All Africa Conference of Churches 1963–1992.* 1997. All Africa Conference of Churches. Nairobi, Kenya.

Werner, Roland, William Anderson, and Andrew Wheeler (eds). *Day of Devastation, Day of Contentment: The History of the Sudanese Church Across 2000 Years.* 2001. Paulines Publications Africa. Nairobi, Kenya.

Additional Resources

Faith-in-Sudan Book Series. A 14-volume series published by Paulines Publications Africa, PO Box 49026, Nairobi, Kenya. [All published since the year 2000; all in print.]

Mbeki, Thabo. *Africa: The Time Has Come.* 1998. Tafelberg Publishers Ltd. 28 Wale Street, Cape Town.

_____. "The African Renaissance, South Africa and the World." April 9, 1998. United Nations University.

Miller, Harold F. "Peace and Reconciliation in Africa." 1996. Occasional Paper. Mennonite Central Committee.

_____. "The Quest for Legitimacy: Church and State in Africa." January 18, 1989. Presentation in Winnipeg, Manitoba, Canada. [Unpublished paper.]

Thompson, V. B. *Africa and Unity.* 1969. Longman. London. [A definitive work on Pan Africanism.]

2
Peacemaking in the Horn of Africa: A Local Initiative

THE SETTING WAS the village of Sade, on the Ethiopian side of the River Daua. Fifty miles to the east, the borders of Somalia, Kenya, and Ethiopia converged, just a few miles from the Kenyan town of Mandera and the Somali town of Bula Hawa. For nearly a hundred miles, the River Daua forms the border between Ethiopia and Kenya, a prominent marker, and for many people a source of life. The whole of the area was long characterized by tensions between the contiguous countries. During the Ogaden War, a Somali military offensive carried out between July 1977 and March 1978 over the disputed Ethiopian region of Ogaden, tensions had been very strong indeed.

As in many African border situations, the populace was torn by multiple loyalties. In Rhamu town, for example, one heard, not atypically, of a family with one son fighting in the Ogaden War on behalf of the Somali government, a second son in the Ethiopian Army, fighting in the same war, and a third son with the Kenya Air Force. Little attempt was made to fudge the anomalies; after all, it was argued, "a man must make a living somehow!"

Next to the district officer's compound in Rhamu was a one-acre enclosure, the site of a service unit maintained by the National Council of Churches of Kenya (NCCK). The houses were constructed with mud and wattle, topped by thatch from the local variety of palm trees. Facilities were simple and straightforward, reflecting the declared aim of providing a Christian presence in this predominantly Muslim community.

The vision for a Christian service unit in Rhamu had been conjured originally by British Quakers. At one point, they had proposed the placement of workers in each of the three countries, with all appointees placed within reasonable proximity of the border area to facilitate comradery and mutual support. The Quaker volunteer in the Ogaden region of Ethiopia left when armed conflict erupted. There had not been time sufficient to arrange for a placement in Somalia. Eventually, Rhamu featured the presence of an Australian couple recruited by the Quakers, administered under the auspices of the NCCK. The Australians lived and worked there for four years, and were then replaced by a British Quaker couple under the same administrative arrangement.

Rhamu was rarely mentioned without reference to the prominent Sheikh Abbas, whose compound was situated approximately two kilometers to the east. He was a recognized Koranic scholar with influence extending far into the hinterlands of the tri-country area. Although he traveled little, more than anyone else in the area he was attuned to the nuances of the day. There was no doubt about his moral authority, wielded effectively by means of a forceful but most congenial personality. During the five years following the establishment of the NCCK service center, he proved a forthright advisor and counselor. His influence was exercised invariably toward the stability of the immediate community and amicable tri-country relationships.

Such were the physical and sociopolitical characteristics of the area around the hamlet of Sade. The Somali people living in the immediate environs were members of the Dogodia clan. They spoke the Somali language and lived scattered in the tri-country area. Among them was a specially recognized person known as the *wabarr*, a traditional leader who represented an intriguing mix of religious and secular concerns: he was a well-informed member of the Muslim faith community, as well as an astute sociopolitical personality.

The father of the incumbent *wabarr* had served as a traditional leader, as had his grandfather. From among several sons, the *wabarr* had been selected by his father because of a prominent birthmark on the side of his torso that was said to resemble Arabic script and was deemed by the father a sign of God's blessing. The father had died thirty-three years earlier, but before his demise he had publicly announced that his son, marked by the sign of God, was to serve as the successor *wabarr*. However, the son was not to assume and exercise his office until he had attained forty years of age.

As might have been anticipated in this tightly knit rural community, the people remembered well the pronouncement of the elder *wabarr*; indeed, long before the official installation of the *wabarr*, they had begun to ask: "Where is the new *wabarr* and why does he not assume his office? How are we to live through these difficult times without the guidance of a leader from among ourselves?" True to his calling, and in response to popular sentiment, the current *wabarr* eventually embraced his responsibility with remarkable aplomb.

Together with his followers, he requested protection from the Ethiopian authorities in the form of a mobile government unit, in the first instance to facilitate his official assumption of the office of *wabarr*. The request was granted, giving form to the strange specter of a Marxist government blessing the enthronement of a traditional religious, socio-ethnic leader. But they could hardly have afforded to do less, for the Somali Dogodia obviously enjoyed strong potential and actual relationships in the cross-border area with their tri-country Somali cohorts.

Installation ceremonies for *wabarr* were celebrated in the scattered border villages, accompanied by much feasting. Within a given village, the festivities extended to four or five days, involving thousands of people, with many animals donated for slaughter and subsequent feasting. Pledges of loyalty took the form of ceremonies in which milk was poured on the new *wabarr*. In turn, the *wabarr* addressed the people and called for peace. Specifically, he called for a cessation of *shifta* (clandestine guerilla) activity. He admonished the *shifta* to surrender their guns and live in peace. On the part of some members of the *shifta* guerilla movement, the response was immediate. Guns were surrendered during the ceremonies. Subsequent reports confirmed that scattered members of the *shifta* continued to heed the call for peace.

Eventually the *wabarr* was properly installed. Meanwhile, direct relationships had developed between the *wabarr* and the NCCK's Rhamu service center. An NCCK staff member from the local Borana community—ethnically akin to the Somali community—and in this case a Christian, had on occasion met the *wabarr*. The NCCK staff member witnessed one of the village peace ceremonies and shared the goodwill intentions with people of Rhamu, and in particular with Sheikh Abbas.

All indicators suggested that the *wabarr* would exercise his office with freedom and strength. In so doing, he would be assuming a stabilization role among Ethiopia's ethnic Somali people, just as Rhamu's Sheikh Abbas had played his role among Kenya's Somali community. It was a hope that inspired nurture and encouragement.

—January 7, 1982

As recounted by John Godhana, a National Council of Churches of Kenya staff member, for a number of years assigned to the NCCK Rhamu service center.

3
The "Food Decade" in Africa

THE SKIES OVER Nairobi, Kenya, were laden with rain. After the most severe drought in forty years, the countryside was green again. Vegetable farmers north of Nairobi had a produce glut on their hands; market prices had dropped below production costs. Although insufficient to meet the country's needs, the wheat harvest in the Rift Valley was alleviating some portion of the food deficits. Bakeries, which had been closed for brief periods, had resumed the baking of bread.

Earlier in the year (1984), Ghana was reported to be in desperate straits. Drought had devastated crops. Relief foods, when they arrived, could not be moved because there was no fuel, no tires, no spare parts. Then the rains had come, confusing market women, who were all set to sell imported foods, but were now undercut by the cheaper, locally produced food. Rains at the wrong time made for bad business. Meanwhile, in Ethiopia, hundreds of thousands of people faced starvation. Media publicity had elicited unprecedented response from both the West and the East. Scores of airplanes had converged on the capital of Addis Ababa, delivering food. According to the media, hunger in Africa had captured the world's imagination.

It was true. People in Africa were dying of hunger. It was unhelpful or inaccurate, however, to paint the whole continent with the same brush of despair. Understanding and eventual action were best based on more careful analysis. As a generalization, it was fair to observe that food production on the continent over the past two decades had fallen below the population growth rate. But the statistics were slippery. In some parts of Africa, food production had risen significantly during the same period—in Kenya, food production on the whole increased even during drought time, allowing Kenya to become a net exporter of agricultural produce. The picture was not one of unmitigated disaster; however, it did not allow for complacency.

Fundamental Shifts

Hunger had been created by all manner of local and worldwide changes, many of them beyond the control of the people, who in consequence became the victims. Some of the shifts were of a fundamental character, having accumulated over time into seemingly intractable problematics. They were subtle and appeared, half-hidden, in the cold statistics of government documents. A 1981 "sessional paper" on food policy produced by the Kenyan government extrapolated trends from past performances and predicted that by 1989 the country would be saddled with structural food deficits—up to 300,000 tons per annum—even in times of adequate rains. What forces were shaping such predictions? Why did they tend toward food deficits and not toward plenty for all?

The Food Decade

While it was too early and probably unfair at the time of this writing to attach a label to the 1980s, labels do at times suggest perspective. In Africa, the 1960s were indisputably the years of "independence," the 1970s the decade of military coups, and the 1980s, perhaps, the decade of "food" (deficits, droughts, starvation, and relief-food shipments). Earlier labels were easily recalled: the slave period, the suppression of slavery, the missionary initiative, the 1884 imperial division of Africa, and so on. Was the whole of the two-hundred-year history of Africa in some perverse sense structured to lead inexorably toward the present food situation? That proposition would clearly be too simplistic, but perhaps a helpful heuristic point nonetheless. Presently, most of the food produced and consumed in Africa derives from peasant farmers. Typically, more than 80 percent of the population in an African country is classified as peasant or subsistence farmers on relatively small scale, involving most or all family members. According to the "ideal" definition of peasant farmers, they were generally believed to be self-sufficient in food, or nearly so. For many, this characterization no longer holds. All over the continent, peasant farmers had entered the world of cash crops, thus becoming newly dependent on larger but also more esoteric support systems, involving government-sponsored extension services, commercial fertilizers, cooperative movements, and international pricing and marketing systems. In Kenya, the maize-growing areas provided people living in the semiarid zones with food; staples had, in some sense, become cash crops. Large mechanized bakeries had delivery trucks scurrying all over the country, feeding the growing taste for bread. According to some observers, this was not the path toward inexpensive food with sufficiency for all, but a production/consumption pattern commensurate with larger market systems.

Peasantization

According to scholars, the peasantization of Africa is a relatively recent phenomenon, and represents one of the last of the great peasant systems of the world. There is much debate about how and whether peasant societies stand to gain from transformation into predictable, regulated agricultural production systems, moving—presumably and hopefully—beyond self-sufficient subsistence to surplus production. So far, attempts at restructuring have not enjoyed much success, the most notable example coming from Tanzania. Soon after achieving independence in 1961, a World Bank-inspired villagization scheme was undertaken. It was said to have failed because of the high capital requirements. Later, on a more ideological basis, the whole of the rural population was shifted—sometimes forcibly—into *Ujamaa* (communal) villages.

In both cases, agricultural production declined as consequence. And when the promised village amenities—piped water, health clinics, formalized agricultural extension services—were not forthcoming, the village people resumed subsistence agriculture. Academics spoke of the government being unable to "capture" peasants for surplus production—to feed the cities. Tanzanian president Julius Nyerere spoke of a peasant obligation to produce more food than was required for subsistence living. But peasants defied official expectations. In one area of Tanzania, they defiantly elected traditional chiefs with the mandate to lead them into some form of traditional subsistence farming. Similar reports came from Ghana. Many areas of Zaire never seriously flirted with cash crops, and over the years have been relatively self-sufficient in food.

At one point, a UNICEF report took note of rising levels of healthy nutrition in areas of Tanzania that had been cut off from the formal or modern sector of the country. A shortage of tires and fuel ensured that trucks did not collect the available staple/cash crops in the villages for shipment to urban areas. In consequence, males in the community had less cash to spend on debilitating brew. And, with buses grounded, they had no way of escaping the village. So they joined women in farming, resulting in improved conditions all around. Meanwhile, people living in the major urban centers of Tanzania had been eating "yellow maize," a euphemism for imported food, generally much less acceptable socially and deemed less tasty than the locally grown white maize.

So far, Africa's peasant agriculture has yielded only reluctantly to analysis and to transformation by prescription. Tanzania's experiments were based in part on a homegrown, more or less benign version of (indigenous) socialism known as *Ujamaa* (familyhood).

Remarkable Production

Coffee, tea, and cotton served as the commodity crops that lent themselves to smallholder ("peasant") production. The resultant production was remarkable. Subsistence peasants were transformed into foreign-exchange earners, food crops became commercialized, individual farmers became specialized, and food tastes accommodated the changes. At best, the system worked reasonably well, though the diet changes tended to create malnutrition. But when drought struck, the system floundered. Dependencies that had taken shape around cash crops in the form of "inputs" became more pronounced. In the absence of a built-in food-storage system, the country was forced to draw on international goodwill as a source of basic staples.

Formidable Issues

For the long term, African agriculture faces formidable issues, including population pressures, ecological degradation, and the unknowns of biotechnology. While there are now indications that population growth around the world may be leveling off, Africa as a continent has not joined the trend. Even more pressing than the aggregate population growth are the burgeoning urban centers, typically expanding at a 10 percent annual rate. Population-control and family-planning measures in Africa have had only marginal effects on the overall patterns. Population trends interact closely with many other factors, most of which are not adequately understood, and while direct action on population growth rates may be desirable, there should be no illusions about its effectiveness.

Ecological issues in Africa are real. Approximately 25 percent of the African continent is well endowed for agriculturally based food production. Most of the remainder is arid, semiarid, or tending in that direction. (It should be noted that semiarid areas do produce vast quantities of meat with remarkable efficiency. Africa's pastoral systems are resilient.) Ethiopia's famine seemed to reflect a combination of severe ecological degradation, following a massive drought, with an admixture of civil disorder. While the immediate drought and civil unrest can eventually be resolved, the long-term and accelerating ecological degradation can be reversed only with enormous effort, if at all. There simply is no escaping the vagaries of ecological degradation. It is there, it will expand, and the cost of dealing with it must be built into the development process on a permanent basis.

Biotechnology

One of the persistent dilemmas faced by the African decision maker has to do with the selection of technology. Given a certain sense of deprivation imposed by the colonial experience, there is an understandable urge among the elite to select the best and the latest technology offered by the industrial world. Currently, a major challenge comes from the field of biotechnology, especially as it affects food- and cash-crop prospects.

Already, several companies in the United States are producing pyrethrum by means of biotechnology. Pyrethrum is the much-praised biodegradable insecticide derived originally from a plant grown most effectively in East Africa. The synthetic counterpart produced in the United States is believed to pose a threat to the viability of pyrethrum as a cash crop in

Africa. But that is only the beginning. According to some forecasts, within the foreseeable future, biogenetic research will open the way for cloning of coffee and tea plants, which can then be grown in controlled environments within the industrialized countries. Sweeteners derived from temperate-zone crops possess the potential of replacing third world sugar production. And there are many other examples.

The actual scientific breakthroughs are only one aspect of the major shifts taking place. Whereas the new strains of wheat, rice, and corn (maize) became available to the world via relatively "open" international research centers, much of the new bioresearch will be carried out by private, multinational companies. Their findings will become private property, open to the privileged who trade on the world's stock markets. At the moment, it is difficult to imagine how African agriculture will play anything but second fiddle to the promises and threats of the biogenetic research explosion now underway in the industrialized nations.

Conflict and Security

Any consideration of the macro food situation in Africa must in some manner touch on the issue of conflict and security. The link between food deficits, hunger, and overt conflict is obvious. Ethiopia became the classic example, but there are others: Angola, Mozambique, Sudan, and, earlier, Somalia. The link between conflict and hunger would seem to have the virtue of being incontrovertible. Less obvious, but just as real, are the tensions inherent in the whole of the "north-south" relationship, which is woven in such a manner that each major international economic hiccup or natural aberration (such as droughts or earthquakes) appears to provide another opportunity to increase any advantage that "north" exercises over "south." Many of those links are, from a northern perspective, the "innocent" public face of "good business." In the south, there are collaborators—usually the elite beneficiaries: middle-level job seekers and jobholders—who settle for a facade of modernity, and the majority who know little about modern-sector workings or why situations become more and more difficult.

A prolonged exposure to a non-industrialized sector of the world leads easily toward subjective empathy for the people who seem to be victims of power plays and structures beyond their control. In reality, things are more complex. Situations of stress abound in contradictions, and Africa at this time is no exception. It is probably naive to assume that any particular perspective is complete, and probably equally naive to assume that any one actor plays more than a small part, whether as culprit or as bearer of remedial solutions.

—1987-1989

This article appeared in *Mandate*, a publication of the United Church of Canada, in an issue entitled "Creation in Crisis: Rural Life in Canada and Africa."

4
Approaches to Grassroots Development

THERE IS AN ASSUMPTION among the purveyors of the development enterprise that somewhere, at some identifiable social level or geographic spot, the change process is taking place in pure form. This is an illusion, of course. Not only are change and development processes elusive; they are multisided and multidirectional. Moreover, there is little agreement regarding the common intent or purpose of these processes, or even a broadly accepted definition of "grassroots development." Nevertheless, the term is intriguing and merits some discussion.

Grassroots development is readily associated with land and landedness, which places the discussion immediately at the heart of Kenya's most sensitive and longstanding political debate. There is, on the one hand, the gut-level felt need for landownership—"a man needs land, if only as a burial site." This need has something to do with "home," with "territoriality," and with "place." By itself, such understanding profoundly affects the price of a piece of land and, by extension, the sociopolitical heat generated around landownership. It is assumed that as the modernization process continues, the primal links with land will slowly be weakened or eroded. Whether this trend is inevitable is central to the continuing discourse on the subject.

On the other hand, market forces seem to indicate clearly that land translates into money—either in the case of a direct sale, or in the form of collateral, or as an economic base from which to produce cash crops. Indeed, as cash crops become more entrenched and as African economies become ever more integrated with the global marketplace, there will be continuing and growing alienation from the land. Ownership will be concentrated in the hands of the few, with production and consumption becoming specialized and commercialized. Such has been the fate of modern agro-economies. To varying degrees, Kenya has aspired to "technologies" that bespeak and embrace Western-style agricultural systems. Adverse effects of this emulation can be countered only by specific and clear intent.

In Kenya, the smallholder farmer manages to survive amid complex social and economic dynamics. Here the consumption of basic food crops is not carefully costed. Cash crops are grown, the income of which provides entry into niches of the formal-sector marketplace. And the conversation is not so much about efficient cash-crop production as it is of turning a relative excess of labor into cash. There may be an encounter with the odd agricultural extension agent, but such consultation will focus primarily on the fine details of growing exotic produce for foreign or modern-sector urban markets. For many smallholder farmers, diets remain more or less "traditional," un-costed, and relatively unchanged. In areas where equity and stability prevail, it can be assumed that diets are also reasonably well balanced nutritionally.

Some variation of this grassroots "ideal type" characterizes significant portions of smallholder farms in the Kenyan highlands. Having been raised on a mixed smallholder farm in the US with a strong sense of self-sufficiency (particularly with regard to food) and only furtive forays into the modern cash sector (via cash crops and sale of labor), I have a strong urge to fix or freeze this model. Here the elements of family and community are reasonably strong. Here one finds varying degrees of ritual and routines still intact. In short, here one tends to be aware of and tends to emphasize social and community strengths. At this more or less ideal grassroots level, what might be the function and focus of the modern development impulse?

In general, the modern formal-sector development enterprise has assumed that the grassroots are deficient in a number of ways. People living and working at the grassroots level are presumed to be at the end of the line: they survive with inadequate access to public services; they will eventually catch up with the modern sector, provided sufficient energies to that end are expended. It is implied that the grassroots have been neglected; that in their undeveloped state, people are deficient in knowledge and skills.

They need, with aid from the modern sector, to be assisted toward an enjoyment of the fruits of independence. Such assumptions do of course beg questions regarding acceptable or affordable norms in modern Kenya. Meanwhile, it has become clear, even to the most casual observer, that vast numbers of people living at grassroots levels of society demonstrate amazing survival stamina. They have survived; they are in the living present; they have succeeded!

It is a matter of some discussion as to whether the rural or grassroots communities function as primary supporters of the urban sectors or whether the urban areas, ostensibly the generators and remitters of cash to rural areas, are keeping momentum at the grassroots viable. This is a false discussion. Obviously, a complex mix of dynamics connects and separates the respective urban from rural realities. These dynamics have been given a variety of names, including the colorful designation "the economy of affection."

This term refers to the invisible ties and dynamics that cause apparently disparate sectors of the social economy or disparate geographic sectors of the country to cohere. It explains how certain commercial ventures fail or succeed in defiance of accepted modern-sector norms.

It explains why people may be "down, but not out." There are always friends and relatives upon whose goodwill credit can be obtained and new beginnings made or minimal survival sustained. Dr. Goran Hyden, the academic who coined the term, tended to view the presumed phenomenon, at least partially, in negative terms. He proposed that the "economy of affection" impeded the growth and rational deployment of modern-sector options. According to him, if a tradition-based rural community was to achieve rapid modern-sector economic development and institutional maturity, then the residual strengths of the "economy of affection" would need to be sacrificed in favor of more rational, predictable ways of economic management.

His proposition was at best problematic. During the immediate postindependence decades, Kenya's overall economic growth kept pace, more or less, with the population growth. This was accomplished by means of a rather vigorous cash-crop sector (coffee, tea, pyrethrum), by growth in the tourism sector, and by the expansion of certain "invisible" earnings—factors that suggested significant structural changes in the economy and shifts commensurate with wealth accumulation. A modern-sector elite had been made visible amid astonishing gains, while at grassroots level there were signs of only modest gains or, in some sectors, stagnation.

In real terms, a certain degree of class formation (differentiation) had taken place. Inasmuch as the entrepreneurial class had consolidated its ability to provide rational leadership for the economy, some of Hyden's concerns had been accommodated even as the lower, poorer echelons of society became increasingly marginalized. But it also appeared that the effective functioning of the "economy of affection" had mitigated the sharpest edges of the most glaring disparities. For example, the well salaried were constantly under pressure to contribute monetarily toward harambee ("let's all pull together") projects, some of which benefited precisely the more marginalized sectors of rural society. Or a senior official in the civil service might assist a junior relative with the establishment of a street-side kiosk offering the basics of milk, tea, and aspirin, among much else, thus in a single gesture meeting an obligation to next of kin newly arrived in town, deflecting a potential dependent, and adding a bit to the GNP! The *jua kali* (informal, open air—literally "hot sun") sector of the economy had expanded dramatically, giving expression to the largesse of the "economy of affection" dynamic. This dynamic cut across rural-urban divides, across geographic divides, and across the informal-formal economic divides. In some ways it had rendered the notion of grassroots delightfully unmanageable! Thus, a pure-form category conforming to the notion of grassroots remained elusive. At this stage in Kenya's development, all sectors of society, whether seen as layers of differentiated income levels or as points on an affluence spectrum, were perforated by the "economy of affection." This was evidenced by the phenomenal routine leakage of what in a more industrialized society would be considered confidential information.

Viewed positively, this characteristic of Kenyan society easily met one of the much-repeated requirements of the development enterprise—namely, ready communication channels. Formal-sector development tended to place a price on information, skills, and technologies. Modern economies can be seen as carefully managed systems of scarcity. On the other hand, informal sectors of the economy—the grassroots end of the spectrum—tended to operate in complex open fashion. Indeed, some indigenous societies placed great value on the broadest possible sharing of all available resources as the ultimate form of social insurance and social justice.

It was widely accepted that agriculture, ranging from subsistence to high-level agri-business, formed the basis of the economy. And, at this point in Kenya's development trajectory, there were still strong emotional and social links between the urban and rural areas of the country. In the context of development discourse, and more particularly in the development efforts of nongovernmental organizations (NGOs), this relationship pattern presented some interesting challenges. Meanwhile, a number of working relationships within the development matrix had evolved, each with its respective merits. The remainder of this essay comprises a brief description of the range of NGO development modalities. But first a word on NGOs as evolving entities.

It is now widely accepted that NGOs make their debut in the context of some disaster, crisis, or stress period. Crises call for immediate action, usually in the form of what is called relief activity. From relief activities there is then a shift toward medium-term or long-term development activity, usually taking the form of projects focused on some specific sector of the social or economic spectrum. In subsequent phases, NGOs move toward specialty roles, or they provide linkages between all manner of institutions.

The linkage or "networking" role is viewed by some observers as the most mature level of the NGO development community. In the absence of any widely accepted NGO development theory, these comments on NGO evolution and changing function must be accepted as tentative. In practice, of course, NGO activities represent a mix of strategies and approaches. Herewith an abbreviated subjective overview in the context of Kenya's peculiar conditions.

In Kenya, both indigenous and foreign NGOs have at various points over the past twenty years engaged in relief activity. Such activities have usually been occasioned by "normal" or, at times, "abnormal" drought. With Kenya changing rapidly during this period, it was probably fair to note that "normal" droughts were increasingly rendered "abnormal" because of more ready media coverage, because of a wider range of response possibilities, and because of the politicization of disparities imposed by the country's diverse weather patterns. Numerous examples of sustained and carefully planned development programs emerged from what were initially emergency relief responses. As a matter of fact, it was accepted that "disaster," one form of which could be instigated by drought, provided the conditions for unusual community cooperation or for unusual collaboration around specific development options by disparate NGOs. In other words, "disaster" situations had repeatedly provided catalyst conditions for major departures toward creative development activity.

It was also accepted that churches, collectively and individually, functioned as part of the far-flung NGO networks in the country. Some of their efforts were collaborative; some were specific and individuated. For example, over a ten-year period (early 1970s to early 1980s), the Catholic Church operated an intense program of adult education and lay mobilization. This constituted, in retrospect, an amazing combination of approaches and techniques, leaving no stone unturned in an effort to move individuals and communities toward self-conscious and self-initiated change. In the end, the initiative was viewed by both church hierarchy and government as a bit too powerful and too effective. Thanks to pressure from both quarters, the program was diversified, domesticated, and in some dioceses, discontinued completely. The story of this strenuous effort has been recorded in a booklet entitled *Go to the People* by Jerry Crowley. That effort provided an example of NGO development affecting grassroots and the highest levels of decision-making in the country, in addition to many layers in between. Importantly, aspects of the techniques championed by the program continued to inform the decision-making dynamics within and outside the Catholic Church.

Since independence in 1963, much of the formal change process in Kenya had taken place within the general "top-down" category. It had been assumed that people needed to be told what to do and how to do it. In its own way, this method had been effective. Inevitably, however, some groups and individuals perceived themselves to have been left outside the development exercise. Examples abound of groups that mobilized themselves for action. In one case, a small community long marginalized ethnically, politically, and ecclesiastically organized itself around its own leadership, decided on its own development priorities, and proceeded toward implementation. Money was collected within the group by means of the traditional round-robin savings scheme, with each member paying a monthly fee. Each month, the whole of the savings would become available to meet the development needs of an individual group member. Eventually, this well-honed traditional process became more refined: the group developed a list of priorities to be pursued by the community, the first of which was a permanent domestic water-storage facility fed by roof catchments. For this purpose, appropriate technology generated by a national NGO was deployed, calling for members of the group to be trained in the relevant skills. Very soon, water collection and storage facilities became available to many homesteads.

In this case, at least some portion of the dynamic that moved the project seemed to emanate from the sense of having been "left behind" or "neglected" by formal development structures. Relevant technology, the group learned, could be gleaned from either formal or informal sources when necessary; this particular water-related technology became relevant primarily in the context of a strong group dynamic and deliberate choice. In short, this bottom-up community effort seemed to have written technology small and group cohesion and creative group dynamics large. Hence the challenge of how best to render available a variety of well-tested, affordable technologies that could be readily mobilized by self-generated, self-motivated groups.

Some discussion in development literature has focused on the possibility of indigenous groups moving from subsistence mutual-aid systems toward what would be recognized as the modern sector. So far, the debate has been inconclusive, though evidence from the grassroots has become increasingly significant. From Burkina Faso came the remarkable story of the Naam Movement, drawing on indigenous socioeconomic forms and functions but applying them toward recognized modern-sector development efforts. Branches of the movement have spread throughout the country. Naam leadership was locally based, investing considerable time in the nurture and the adaptation of indigenous practice to modern possibilities. As it happened, the national political leadership in Burkina Faso espoused a strong sense of a national self-help ethos, thus lending support to Naam. In this case, the Naam Movement was deemed to be an NGO effort, offering both national umbrella and grassroots functions. For any foreign NGO active in such a situation, there would be the ready possibility of widespread dissemination of technologies. A prior requirement for the foreign, supporting NGO would be to recognize the validity of Naam as an authentic, local NGO entity.

From Zimbabwe, there came the example of the Organization for Rural Associations for Progress (ORAP), a grassroots development organization. Here, in contrast to Burkina Faso, the movement had not always enjoyed the blessing of the government. This was partly because of political cleavage between the dominant ethnic groups in the country (ORAP is based in the minority "opposition" area of Zimbabwe) and partly because a strong top-down formal sector had been inherited from the colonial period. The leadership of ORAP, as in the case of Naam, was local, but unlike Burkina Faso, drew only indirectly on indigenous structures for its administrative format. In the early stages of the project, leadership was undertaken largely by women. ORAP had committed itself to a strong diet of debate and dialogue, focused both on the theoretical basis of development and generally on development methodology. With regard to the former there was a return to rural cultural roots, this in an attempt to neutralize the alienation so strongly imposed by an extended colonial period. Thus, ORAP looked to indigenous values for its "spiritual" inspiration, and to a variety of local and overseas donor NGOs for an exchange of ideas on methodologies and technologies, the latter on an as-needed, as-appropriate basis. Again, as in the case of Naam, there was maneuvering space for an array of support and linkage engagement with a variety of both local and international NGOs.

How are such creative groups or these kinds of dynamics generally identified? From several directions, growing interest was directed at what could be called the fine art of inventory. As increasing recognition was accorded to the viability of the semi-subsistence smallholder farmer, there was the commensurate development of tools for purposes of identification and inventorizing. A long-time development practitioner in Kenya developed an extensive checklist designed to identify the overall social and economic value of the smallholder enterprise. Some of this information was presented in economic terms, some in sociological or ecological terms. So far, the greater NGO community has made relatively little use of such analytical tools and has given even less attention to the possibility of devising its own range of inventory tools. This would seem to be particularly urgent in a country where the informal sector is large and remarkably strong, but also mostly unquantified and ignored. Additionally, such a role would seem to mesh admirably with what has been alluded to as the "mature" NGO networking function.

As suggested in the early part of this reflection, Kenya comprised a grand mix of formal and informal economic sectors. Everyone, it seemed, nurtured some sense of rural linkages, though this sense varied considerably and was probably, over the long term, on the wane. The linkages between these diverse sectors on the spectrum were explained to some degree by what has been called the "economy of affection." Contrary to what certain development theory holds—namely, that the "economy of affection" served as a development impediment—here the case is being made that these myriad informal ties can be fed and nurtured in creative ways for multidirectional, multilayered development. The challenge to the NGO community was precisely that of recognizing the fluidity of the situation and devising tools of support that meshed with and enhanced the potential change dynamics. Here the networking model came into its own. It worked within a nonhierarchical structure in which form and content converged increasingly into lean, well-honed function.

The networking mode assumes that there are many senders, receivers, and sharers of information. It assumes that these participants are compelled by the urgency and the relevance of the information being communicated rather than being enamored of the status conferred by structure or hierarchy. Furthermore, the networking mode assumed that useful information could be inserted into the communication network at any point along a vast continuum, with the assurance that it would reach and be appropriated by appreciative hosts and consumers of the information.

Obviously, not just any kind of information would do. Here one is identifying information that NGOs handle best, certainly not highly technical treatises. One was talking about technologies that featured the virtue of wide applicability, a short lead time for skill acquisition, and relatively quick, visible results. One was also talking of information sharing that eluded the tendency toward monopolies—a tendency that would again render information scarce, precisely what the NGO community wished to avert.

For the present and for the near future, Kenya can be thought of as a grassroots society, differentiated into a wide spectrum of functions. NGOs would do well to acknowledge the existing informal networks within the country, feeding them with relevant, useful information, but in bureaucratically disinterested fashion. Such a posture calls for more than the usual creativity, though it is premised on the emergence of a productive pluralist economy.

—November 1986

5
Food Politics in Africa

THE POLITICS OF FOOD reflect, essentially, the politics of development. Development as a change or modernizing process has in turn been informed by a variety of models adopted from the Western, industrialized world.

Colonialism in Africa was many things to many people. Under the weight of its own internal contradictions, colonialism succumbed to the "independence years" of the 1950s and 1960s. African participation in world wars on behalf of colonial powers and the exposure to Western education raised expectations with regard to freedom and independence across the continent. Cities came to symbolize the promise that was development. It was there that those exposed to formal Western-style education became accustomed to and took on Western lifestyles.

The 1960s were known as the First Development Decade, so declared by the United Nations Organization. This was a period devoted to the quest for rapid change with measurable rates of economic growth. United Nations agencies, together with a host of voluntary, nongovernmental agencies, joined the effort. In retrospect, it was a decade of remarkable mobilization.

Underlying the whole of this change process, and to a significant extent guiding the process, was the assumption that industrialization served as a "development engine." After all, Western nations were developed, and they could almost uniformly be characterized as industrialized. In their expansive advice, planners and development experts reflected such assumptions. No national plan was considered complete without at least an approving nod in the direction of a budding mini-industrial sector.

The 1970s, the Second Development Decade, witnessed an explosion of global awareness. It was an awareness informed by more than a dozen

United Nations conferences on issues such as housing, food, environment, deserts, health, water, and energy. Many of these conferences spawned follow-up structures with monitoring facilities and action programs. Such follow-up initiatives exposed a growing awareness that the earth in fact contained limited resources. They were also an indication that accepted development models were infused with errant possibilities.

In general, the conferences demonstrated that Western change models were in fact too expensive for uniform blanket implementation around the world. To be fair, the conference series had searched for and tentatively identified at least one alternative development model, notably in health care. In its 1978 conference in Alma Ata, USSR, the World Health Organization (WHO) officially coined the concept of primary health care. As an alternative development model, it drew inspiration from the Chinese ("barefoot doctor") experience, at the time a distinctly non-Western healthcare model. As a radical departure from generally accepted development norms, that initiative by the WHO remains unique.

Not only were the change models deployed during the two initial development decades (the 1960s and 1970s) deficient or unwieldy; they also produced some unanticipated side effects. Most conspicuously, the development process seemed to lead inexorably to food deficits. More dramatically, food deficits appeared in precisely those countries "blessed" with salable minerals such as oil, bauxite, or iron ore, easily traded for industrial or consumer goods. A country like Nigeria with its oil reserves shifted from being a major exporter to Africa's largest importer of food. Oil replaced food as the chief foreign-exchange spinner. Across Africa the pattern became familiar.

Even countries like Kenya, which was not exporting mineral wealth, made dramatic shifts in their productive bases. The development ethos required that prime agricultural land be committed to the production of commodity cash crops such as coffee, tea, and pyrethrum. Even traditional food crops in developing economies tended to become cash crops, maize being a prime example. In consequence, both cash crops and traditionally grown food crops were sold in international markets in exchange for so-called hard currency, a process pursued at the expense of adequate foods for local consumption. In Kenya, some 50 percent of the foreign exchange so earned was required just to keep the young economy supplied with sufficient petroleum products.

Not only had it become clear that some countries had traded in their food production capacity for a reliance on oil or other mineral exports; it soon became obvious that the basic elements related to food sufficiency had been overlooked during the initial development decades. Food, like air, it had been assumed, would simply "be there." And, except for extensive droughts in certain areas, it usually was.

But as the development process became more entrenched, food deficits became more common. Indeed, they became the norm, accompanied by food aid programs. It was a norm aided and abetted by growing population pressures and commensurate pressures on the remaining arable land.

Early on in the independence experience, many African countries had committed vast sums of money toward the modernization of their agricultural sectors, an exercise commonly expressed in terms of tractor hire schemes, state farms, and extension services in support of cash crops. A review of those early attempts reveals few success stories. Indeed, many of those efforts proved to be little more than huge sinkholes for expensive, borrowed capital funds.

Over time, it became clear that by far the largest portion of the continent's food was in fact produced by smallholder or peasant farmers. Ironically, the peasant farmers were usually the last people to benefit from modern agricultural inputs. They continued to produce food in spite of, and possibly in some cases *because* of, the absence of modern agricultural extension services.

Not only had peasant farmers been overlooked as the prime producers of food; they had been viewed frequently by the development establishment as the problem to be solved. They represented a sector of society deemed to be conspicuously behind the times. If they were to progress at all, they would need to learn to consume fertilizers, to follow extension advice from university-trained officers, and generally to aspire and move toward urban-oriented lifestyles.

Food politics came full circle. Notably absent from the initial development dynamic, food had moved to center stage. In some measure, Africa's political fortunes stood or fell on the basis of available food. The resultant food-aid programs proved to be a mixed blessing. Tanzania served as a case study. The country had discovered, belatedly, that it was host to a voracious grain borer that had caught a ride from its native Central America in a food-aid shipment. With no natural enemies in Tanzania, the insect was doing its destructive work efficiently and effectively, assuring, meanwhile, that the concern for food sufficiency would continue as one of the country's dominant agendas.

At the other end of the spectrum were those African countries that had already arrived at a medium stage of development. Countries such as Uganda, Ghana, and Zaire, with ailing modern sectors, managed somehow to survive. In the case of Uganda, survival was maintained with something of a flair. Among the countries in East Africa, Uganda was the only one featuring net food-export ability, though its basic infrastructure was in a state of extreme disrepair. In other words, with no fertilizers, no tractors, no spare parts, no agricultural extension services, and rationed fuel for transport, the Ugandan peasant farmer produced a food surplus. It was a situation not easily explained by modern development theory.

As expected, many African governments found themselves responding afresh to food deficits. There was talk of establishing clear food policies and of ensuring food sufficiency as a prime concern. Pricing mechanisms were reexamined and grain stores built. And for some countries, the quest for food security constituted a race with population pressures. For others it represented a fundamental shift in the respective approaches to and understandings of development. For all, it was a return to the basics after an initial period of ready flirtation with the industrial-development model.

While governments were obviously major players in the food arena, the supplementary roles of nongovernmental organizations (NGOs) and, in particular, the Christian churches had proven important. To be sure, their contributions had not been uniform. They were guided by extended debates on the relative merits of the spiritual versus the social mission of the churches. Even when churches became actively committed to rural or agricultural initiatives, the involvement was usually implemented by means of expensive Western change and development instruments. Not surprisingly, these took the form of expatriate expertise, rural training institutions, and the intricately conceived project, dependent on foreign monetary support. Missionary-founded churches had all along been seen as the initial benefactors and the wielders of Western educational and health facilities. For many, formal education provided the ticket from rural to urban areas. It was the fickle promise of a job in the modern sector. It invoked the "right" to conspicuous consumption. Probably more than any other Westernizing dynamic, formal education allowed the churches to become embarrassed about the peasants, and to overlook their basic contribution, both as a source of foodstuff and as a source of survival traditions.

Thus, if there was to be fresh thinking and planning with regard to food production, there would need to be dramatically fresh thinking about the peasant farmer. And among those who would be doing their homework in this regard were the churches, for they had been prime movers in the change process; they had functioned, strangely, both as cause and effect.

On the African continent, peasants produce the largest portion of the available food. They represent a collectivity of people with a remarkable mastery of survival techniques related to the husbandry of food varieties, to the vagaries of soil and climate, and to the general diversities of the ecological order. Modern development systems and technologies have hardly begun to account for the creative skills of the African peasant farmer. At worst, that farmer has been ignored. At best, that farmer has been slotted in the name of development into varying degrees of manageable uniformity—delicate, finely tuned systems that, if they break down, provide the shape and dimensions for recurring food deficits.

The nature of the current development order has been such that few African governments have been able to mount an effective challenge. Development aid begets the need for more development aid. Dependencies grow exponentially. The formal sectors of many African economies are no longer operating by established development rules. Informal sectors keep the population majorities alive.

During the past two decades, the political question has been: How is the peasant to be captured as a productive factor in the formal sector of a given economy? To a significant extent, the question has been answered by peasant withdrawal from the formal sector. And the result has been an increasingly productive traditional or informal sector. For policymakers, the situation presents dilemmas. If modern African governments are to govern, they will need to be able to wield control over all the productive sectors of the economy. Until now, the instruments of control have been primarily formal, Western in origin, effectively keeping the peasant at arm's length. It is a matter that has been recognized and addressed only in general terms.

Much of the world of traditional food production and consumption remains unexplored. If food is to be plentiful in Africa, it will be necessary to take a completely fresh approach to the continent's food-producing capacity. It may be necessary to identify and deploy non-Western tools to strengthen the peasant sector. It is reasonable to assume that food sufficiency in the future will be predicated, in some measure, on food traditions from the past. Whether African governments can muster the political will to recognize the primary resources in hand provides a measure of the likelihood of food self-sufficiency in the future.

—Nairobi, March 1982

Note: The above piece was published in an undated edition of the *AACC Bulletin*, Vol. XII No. 1, under the theme "Churches' Commitment to Development," published by the All Africa Conference of Churches, Nairobi, Kenya.

6
Appropriate Technology: A Candle in the Dark?

Modern man does not experience himself as part of nature, but as an outside force destined to dominate and conquer it. He even talks of a battle with nature, forgetting that, if he won the battle, he would be on the losing side.
—Denis Goulet

IS THE DARKNESS alluded to in the title simply inappropriate technology or is it the context within which the various technologies evolve, live, compete, and die? Is the candle as a source of wisdom slowly melting into dribbles of misshapen wax or is it the source (opportunity) from which other candles are to be lit, thus eventually dispelling the darkness of inappropriateness?

Did appropriate technology (A.T.), as understood and promoted by a generation of NGOs during the first (1960s) and second (1970s) UN-declared development decades, have the slightest possibility of making an impact in a world dominated by technological conglomerates, or, in biblical terms, a world dominated by "the powers"? Was it worth anyone's effort to promote or to be concerned with the propagation of A.T.? Did A.T. offer any kind of window onto the development scene, whether in the "north" or in the "south" of our common planet?

Defined in its simplest terms, technology is a multiplier of production (Goulet 1985, 12). The term *appropriate technology* would seem to imply that considerations other than those of a purely technical nature inform the selection or deployment of a particular technology. Like many others caught up in the development fervor of the 1960s and 1970s, my general awareness was invaded by the term, and was focused with the help of *Small Is Beautiful: Economics as if People Mattered* by E. F. Schumacher. A reading of this book constituted a virtual rite of passage for my age-group of development workers. The book's title, like the term appropriate technology, constituted an addition to the English lexicon. During the 1960s and 1970s, the term appropriate technology was added to a pantheon of concepts and ideas such as primary health care, the de-schooling of society, conscientization, and liberation theology, recognized as elements of the alternative-development toolkit.

Like many others, I became involved with the conceptualization and implementation of projects located generally within the designation appropriate technology. Thus the operative development budget of the day typically included a catchall appropriate technology line item in support of readily recognized period pieces, such as windmills, biogas units, ox-drawn equipment, fuel-efficient stoves, and solar voltaic panels. Misadventures quickly cluttered the arena of development initiatives.

An expatriate engineer at the University of Nairobi, with the assistance of a dexterous missionary engineer, was committed to the reinvention of the windmill using the machine tool facilities of an industrial training school in the city. From the outset, there was rarely agreement among the engineers regarding optimal windmill design, while the development costs of the project kept rising far beyond the original projections. On the grounds of the University of Nairobi, just behind the Faculty of Engineering's machine shop, the rusting hulks of the various windmill prototypes could be seen years later, testimony to abandoned technological ventures.

Subsequently, another windmill project took shape across the arid lands of northern Kenya. "Technology speaks for itself; it is its own best advertisement," proclaimed the promotional slogan guiding this project. Several of the windmills installed during the project period did indeed survive for a number of years despite irregular or deficient servicing and the steady disappearance of framework bolts to service the body-decoration needs of local residents.

News of this emerging project had meanwhile spread to neighboring Tanzania. At one point, representatives from USAID and from a prominent American NGO requested the windmill project manager in Kenya to assist with a proposed windmill project in central Tanzania. For this project, a configuration of windmills and small-scale vegetable gardens was envisioned, with the former drawing water from nearby shallow wells to irrigate the latter. The expatriate windmill expert from Kenya walked onto the scene in Tanzania just as Australian windmill engineers were abandoning a recently initiated project that had featured top-of-the-line Southern Cross (Australian) windmills, having attempted in vain for eight years to render them operational. Our expert from Kenya read the signals, despaired of the proposed windmill project for which he had been engaged as advisor, and proceeded on a year-long project-design reconfiguration, eschewing the central windmill component in favor of basic bucket-and-rope technology. Water thus extracted from shallow wells was intended to be hand-flicked onto the small garden plots…roughly what the farmers had been doing before the windmill project was originally conceived!

During this same period, the UK-based Intermediate Technology Development Group (ITDG) was supporting, in yet another project, the design and manufacture of a commercially viable windmill in Kenya. In preparation for the actual manufacturing process, statistical comparisons were made between African wind regimes and those of the vast open plains of Australia or their equivalent in the midwestern United States, whence mainstream windmill design had emerged. In consequence, it was determined that Africa's more diverse wind regimes called for considerable modification in windmill design, more congruent with African meteorological conditions. Eventually, both the costs and the requisite technological sophistication of the new windmills escalated dramatically, such that the prototype could no longer be characterized either as "appropriate" or "affordable" on a commercial basis to the low-income African farmer. Subsequently, this project became marginally viable when the World Bank and well-endowed NGOs lined up as customers to purchase the windmills, making them available on a grant or subsidized basis to a variety of rural community initiatives.

Within the relatively delimited arena of East Africa, A.T. had become identified early on with a narrow, not particularly appropriate range of technological gadgets. This category of technology was isolated, almost completely, from other social and development policy dynamics. Kenya's subsequent promotion of *jua kali* (informal sector) technology did achieve significant success, but the genealogical link between "appropriate" and *"jua kali"* technology was neither sequential nor direct.

By way of a more general comment, technology is destined to function according to the intents of the designer. Hence basic questions persisted: Which values give direction to technology development? Who dreams up the designs and the ensuing technology deployment trajectory? Were technology choices and applications informed by marketplace dictates that had in turn been created and manipulated by "the powers"? What were the functions of creativity and utility in the choice and design of technology? Was there a place for ethical considerations and for some degree of popular participation in this technological quest?

Over the years, the NGO development community was preoccupied with the choice of suitable nomenclature with which to describe the major divides by which our world was living. At the time of this writing, the terminology of "north-south" was in vogue, even as the ideological Cold War language of "east-west" was becoming spurious. The term "third world" had become pejorative. Later accepted parlance referred to the world's divides as "developing/industrializing" versus "developed/industrialized" nations. But the debate regarding appropriate nomenclature continued, if only because the most developed/industrialized nations were also becoming the greatest polluters, rendering them expensive, "unviable fellow passengers" (Schumacher's term) on planet earth. According to one community of political scientists, informed by yet another line of ideological reckoning, the world could readily be divided into peripheries and centers; between cores and margins. Ideological, technological, and economic power accumulated in centers, while people on the peripheries were rendered or deemed powerless.

Was anyone really expecting that technology—large or small, appropriate or inappropriate—would lead to the golden age, bridging the disparities? Technology of whatever kind might well constitute a necessary condition for the attainment of the development to which peoples of the world aspire, but never a sufficient one. According to rumor, even Bill

Gates endorsed this truism. Thus, if in our metaphor A.T. is the candle, what of the darkness? Of what does it consist?

Perhaps the darkness consists of the context in which technology functions—until now a context assumed to be self-evident, comprising the world of efficiencies, production, consumption, and financial bottom lines. If technology is to serve the needs of people, it requires more than the stimulus of the creative turn of phrase. It requires a maximally participatory context, engaging people who will be positively or negatively affected by design and policy choices related to technology. Technologies do not function in economic or policy vacuums. In this regard, George McRobie set out a helpful but not well tested trajectory followed by creative or alternative technology. In his book *Small Is Possible*, he made the assumption that creativity functions on the margins of the mainstream with an expectation that creative technological innovations would be rejected during the initial stages of experimentation and propagation. General acceptance by governments or international institutions he perceived as a second step, while the third step included active involvement (by whom?) on a considerable scale to mobilize technological choices. In a fourth stage, the application of creative technology would become distanced from the "alternative" or "exceptional" nature of the particular technology under consideration. In other words, according to McRobie's scenario, a technological innovation could be expected to move from the creative esoteric periphery through several stages into the mainstream, but in that process—all things being equal and generally positive—it would have had the effect of "humanizing" or mitigating the standard or the prevailing mainstream technology.

During the "development decades," a steady stream of Intermediate Technology Development Group (ITDG) staff from the UK passed through Nairobi on their annual migrations to the tropics. Nearly all of them were technicians and specialists. I always asked them, "Has ITDG launched a search mission for another Fritz Schumacher; for another conjurer of concepts as potent as the original, magical phrase 'small is beautiful'?" Of course that was asking for too much. But it was a way of keeping alive the question: "Does technology, especially *appropriate* or *small* technology, lead its own creative life without the stimulus of the creative turn of phrase from the engineer and philosopher or the open-ended tinkering of a village-based inventor?"

During those creative decades, the ITDG did in fact manage to inform its efforts with a wide range of philosophical and ethical considerations, and with a genuine awareness of how human communities function. In some fashion, the process seemed indeed to follow the four steps as outlined by George McRobie. On the other hand, viewed from almost any perspective, the development enterprise eventually reached certain impasses. Was this because A.T. had not been given sufficiently free rein? Was it too early to assess results or were the centers of technology so overpoweringly efficient in their ability to co-opt that they eventually rendered all technologies mainstream and thus beholden to the political dynamics of the marketplace?

The seminar in which these thoughts were originally shared had been convened in the United States, a country that had at one time assigned more than half of its scientists to research military hardware and software—international power politics guiding technology. There is a stark difference between that posture and the world of my boyhood. I was born and grew to adulthood in rural Amish and Mennonite communities where technology was deliberately appropriated, designed, or bent to serve the expressed values and needs of community. To this day, some Amish communities prescribe for themselves the acceptable size or complexity of a mechanical enterprise or the acceptable degree of mechanization in their farming or manufacturing operations. As a community, they defied the inherent dictates of technology. According to them, the values of a living community must determine the choices with regard to acceptable technology.

People from "developing countries" can recount any number of stories about technology-dumping from the "developed countries"—uneconomic technologies, super-sophisticated (and therefore dependency-creating) technologies, inappropriate technologies, and, all too often, non-participatory technologies. Over time, people in "developing countries" have become aware that technologies are by definition not ethically, economically, or politically neutral.

Item: Biotechnology has been heralded as the gateway to all kinds of material sufficiency for the future. And indeed, over time, there seemed to be promise in spectacular new technological breakthroughs. Modern scientists have the ability to isolate and transpose critical genetic characteristics from one organism to another, or even from one species to another, a facility that translates in the marketplace of North America into commercial genetic patenting, and thence formidable influence in the global marketplace. Both African and North American scientists are entranced by the possibilities and promises of biotechnology.

However, thoughtful African scientists such as Florence Wambugu, a Kenyan genetic engineer, insisted on both the right and the duty of being positively engaged with the biotech debate: "Kenya and other African nations that are rich in genetic resources now have a chance to participate effectively in the biotechnology revolution instead of waiting to be consumers" (Wambugu 2005). Alas, the playing field in this regard was not level. Meanwhile, debate continued regarding the international protocols guiding access to the flora and fauna of Africa where critical raw material ingredients are located. Aware of the disparities, African researchers, scientists, lawyers, legislators, and students of public polity are working frantically to establish infrastructure on the basis of which some semblance of equitable interaction can take place.

Item: For a long time after gaining political independence, Kenya had no legal facility for patenting its own endemic resources, whether technological or genetic. A committed Kenyan inventor or scientist was destined to follow the existing legal provisions to obtain a patent for some innovation, only to be rewarded with a British patent! Like many other examples that could be cited, this one underscored the point that initiatives and technologies from outside Africa had demonstrated their power to define the context of the continent's resources (Juma, 179–207).

Technologies do not stand on their own. Like any form of organized knowledge, technologies "risk mistaking themselves for the whole." They function within contexts that are in turn controlled by a range of politics, policies, markets, and legal systems. Given these realities, what is the function of development workers concerned with ethics in the propagation of

A.T.? Are they called to curse the darkness and light many A.T. candles? Can development workers accept the challenge to address the whole of the context within which A.T. functions, recognizing context as the space within which to participate in the choice of applied technologies?

In the mid-twentieth-century ethical debate, Schumacher, Ellul, and Goulet were considered somber, excessively skeptical commentators on the world's pell-mell embrace of modern technology. A generation later, in the new century, the focus of the conversation intensified dramatically and shifted to both the technological centers and technological peripheries of the world.

In the real world of "the powers," neither lofty philosophical understandings nor the imperatives of technology choices function in neutral space. In this regard, President Thabo Mbeki of South Africa traced the trajectory of technology shifts since World War II, demonstrating that US support for the techno-industrial development of the so-called tiger economies of Southeast Asia was driven not by the marketplace, but by the dictates of Cold War politics (Mbeki 2005, 30–34).

Given that the African metaphysics has all along assumed the unity of all things, the implications for technological candle-lighting on the continent are complex, but also promising. African philosophical self-understanding would seem to assume that the exercise of human agency creates time, space, and all manner of living relationships. Development workers, change agents by whatever designation, together with *wananchi* (ordinary citizens), are called to engagement with the creation and choice of futures. They do so by "lighting candles in darkness," discerning, eliciting, affirming, and mobilizing the dynamics of diversity in the context of a living community. Human well-being is contingent upon the degree of our common self-awareness and upon the degree to which human communities take responsibility for choices, including choices regarding technology, which affect the quality and sustainability of the natural environment for the well-being of all.

Addendum: The above was written in 1988. Since then, Kenya has engaged with numerous technological innovations. By far the most conspicuous has to do with the cell phone. Well over half of Kenya's forty-two million people possess and use cell phones—at any one time, approximately half of the pedestrians on a typical Nairobi street are talking on their cell phones. Kenyans deploy cell phones at a blistering statistical pace to transfer money to each other; to send "air time" to each other; to obtain and service loans; and to activate specialty apps such as iCow, designed to streamline and maximize the reproductive cycle of cattle, among other innovative uses.

One of Africa's largest windfarms is being installed, promising to meet up to a third of the country's electricity needs. Biogas facilities are now available to service the energy and fertilizer requirements of a small-scale dairy farmer or the waste disposal and energy generation required by a medium-sized municipality. Solar panels are being produced in Kenya, available to meet the lighting needs of the small two-room rural dwelling or the energy needs of a modern hotel. Thanks to participatory initiatives undertaken by members of rural communities, hundreds of sand dams in Kenya's semiarid zones and in other African countries provide access to water by means of the most basic no-moving-parts technology: they facilitate ecological conservation, function as bases for economic ventures into market gardening, and augment rural food resources.

In another context, creative young Kenyans assemble around a concept and a place known as iHub, where a profusion of people-friendly technological applications are being developed. "Seeds of Hope," an insert in the Saturday *Nation* newspaper, features innovations by peri-urban entrepreneurs who maximize hands-on production of milk, eggs, meat, fruit, vegetables, honey, furniture, and pottery, among much else. This newspaper feature has gone viral, stimulating the emergence of an equivalent feature in the rival *Standard* newspaper and support services from Egerton University. Even the most casual observer cannot fail to be impressed by the creative and innovative energy on display on every hand in modern Kenya. By some calculations, Kenya now ranks as a middle-income country, even while distressing disparities between the rich and the poor persist. A growing middle class expends its salaries in an ever-growing number of shopping malls; more than seven thousand motor vehicles enter the country every month in support of persistent traffic jams; ecological stress becomes ever more apparent; multistory apartment blocks proliferate; professional, industrial, agricultural, and handicraft skills realize ever greater sophistication; universities proliferate, producing astonishing numbers of graduates. Virtually every aspect of modern life in Kenya can be prefaced with words such as "more," "growth," and "expansion," extending into positive as well as negative dimensions.

With the rest of the world, Kenya is adopting the seventeen UN-endorsed Sustainable Development Goals (SDGs), following the expiry of the earlier Millennium Development Goals (MDGs). In the context of these circumstances, technology of whatever choice functions as a necessary but never a sufficient ingredient in the well-being of a modern nation. It serves most *appropriately* under the vigilance of an engaged human community, for "We have the freedom needed to limit and direct technology; to devise intelligent ways of developing and limiting our power; and to put technology at the service of another type of progress, one which is healthier, more human and more social, more integral" (Pope Francis, address to US Congress on September 24, 2015).

—*May 1988 to September 2015*

Note: An earlier version of this reflection was prepared for an Appropriate Technology Workshop in Washington, D.C. (May 6-8, 1988), sponsored by Servants in Faith and Technology.

Sources

Arbab, Farzam. "Promoting a Discourse on Science, Religion, and Development" in *The Lab , the Temple, and the Market* by Sharon M. P. Harper (ed). 2000. Kumarian Press Inc. Connecticut.

"Choosing Technology for a Healthier Environment." A Shell Oil advertisement in collaboration with CNN's Principal Voices series. *TIME*. February 21, 2005.

Drabek, Anne Gordon. "Development Alternatives: The Challenge for NGOs" in *World Development*, Vol. 15 Supplement. 1987.

Ellul, Jacque. *The Technological Society*. 1965. Knopf. New York.

Goulet, Denis. "The Global Development Debate: The Case for Alternative Strategies" in *Peace and Development*, Vol. 6. Autumn 1985.

_____. *The Uncertain Promise: Value Conflicts in Technology Transfer*. 1989. New Horizons Press (an imprint of the Council on International and Public Affairs). New York.

_____. "Three Rationalities in Development Decision-making" in *World Development*, Vol. 14, No. 2. 1986.

Juma, Calestous. *The Gene Hunters*. 1988. Zed Press. London.

Korten, D. C. "Third Generation NGO Strategies: A Key to People-Centered Development" in *World Development*, Vol. 15 Supplement. 1987.

Mbeki, Thabo. "Africa, The Truth and the Asian Miracle." *New African*. March 2005.

McRobie, George. *Small Is Possible*. 1982. Abacus. London.

Monbiot, George. "Mocking All Our Dreams." *Mail & Guardian*. February 18-24, 2005.

Wambugu, Florence. "Parliament Should Revisit Bio-Tech Bill." *Daily Nation*. March 17, 2005.

Williams, George. "A Protestant Contribution to the Theory and Practice of the Ecumenical Dialogue" in *Voluntary Associations: A Study of Groups in Free Societies* by D. B. Robertson (ed). 1966. John Knox Press. Richmond, VA.

Additional Resources

Buckland, Jerry. *Ploughing Up the Farm: Neo-liberalism, Modern Technology and the State of the World's Farmers*. 2004. Fernwood Publishing (Zed Books). Winnipeg, Manitoba.

Carr, Marilyn. *The AT Reader—Theory and Practice in Appropriate Technology*. 1985. Intermediate Technology Publications. Croton-on-Hudson, New York.

Darrow, Ken, Kent Keller, and Rick Pam. *Appropriate Technology Sourcebook*, Vol. 2. 1981. Volunteers in Asia. Stanford, CA.

George, Susan. *A Fate Worse Than Debt: A Radical New Analysis of the Third World Debt Crisis*. 1988. Viking Penguin Inc. New York.

Goulet, Denis. "Creating Wealth or Causing Poverty?" in *Ethics and the Multinational Enterprise* by W. Michael Hoffman, Anne E. Lange, and David A. Fedo (eds). Conference proceedings, October 10-11, 1985. University Press of America.

_____. "Culture and Traditional Values in Development" in *The Ethics of Development: The Pacific in the 21st Century* by Susan Stratigos and Philip J. Hughes (eds). 1987. University of Papua New Guinea Press. Port Moresby.

Juma-Okande, Mercy. "Move Over MDGs (Millennium Development Goals), Here Come the SDGs (Sustainable Development Goals)." *Daily Nation*. September 30, 2015. Nairobi, Kenya.

Koyama, Kosuke. *Waterbuffalo Theology*. 1974. SCM Press Ltd. London.

Pratt, Brian, and Jo Boyden (eds). *The Field Directors' Handbook: An OXFAM Manual for Development Workers*. 1985. The Oxford University Press. Oxford.

Ramesh, Jairam and Charles Weiss, Jr. (eds). *Mobilizing Technology for World Development*. 1979. Praeger for ODC. New York.

Schumacher, E. F. *Small Is Beautiful: Economics as if People Mattered*. 1973. Harper and Row. New York.

Singer, Hans. *Technologies for Basic Needs*. 1982. International Labor Office. Geneva.

"Synthesis of the African National Reports" in *The Image of Africa; International Exchange on Communication and Development between Africa and Europe*. February 1-5, 1988. Rome.

Volti, Rudi. *Society and Technological Change*. 1988. St. Martin's Press. New York.

7
Reflections on the Rural Development Program of the National Council of Churches of Kenya (1974–1981)

ON NOVEMBER 13, 1961, a meeting was convened by the Christian Council of Kenya's Relief, Research Resettlement Committee at the Limuru Conference Center to consider why there have been recurrent famines, and to see if there was any positive way that churches could participate in farmer training centers that were being envisaged in the service of countrywide settlement schemes. Those deliberations led eventually to the formation of the multi-pronged rural development program of the National Council of Churches of Kenya (NCCK).

I. Introduction

There are many ways of reflecting on any particular experience. Typically, reflection could take the form of a catalogue of details regarding time, place, and cost. It could take the form of an evaluation: it was good, it was bad, it was irrelevant. I choose to reflect on seven years with the NCCK's Rural Development Department from the perspective of "secretary" (responsible administrator) by recording impressions—subjective, general, and more or less random.

It would be presumptuous for any one person to take credit (or for that matter, blame) for the successes and failures of activities and projects pursued. Ideas, initiatives, and skills came from many quarters. Dutch, British, Australian, American, Italian, and Canadian personnel, together with Kenyans from a variety of backgrounds, were all part of the action.

Initiatives launched and implemented by this motley corps were in turn funded from multiple sources, on disparate terms of service and within a variety of relational and administrative structures. Even though the approaches to the range of projects were not uniform, a common thread tied them together. In all cases, the activities represented an attempt to respond to the needs of diverse communities in Kenya and to stimulate their potential, thus rendering life "abundant" (John 10:10).

This reflection constitutes a stroll with the NCCK's Rural Development Department during a seven-year period (1974–1981), halting along the way to savor this or that project or idea. In fact, the stroll will be more or less systematic in terms of sequence, but it is not intended as an exhaustive, detailed review or evaluation of the activities and projects pursued during those years. If this reflection remembers and illumines the obscure point, and provides context and continuity for a range of seemingly disconnected initiatives, it will have served its purpose.

Within the NCCK context, there was, in the first instance, the scope provided by the national character of its mandate and the constituency structure of its membership. There was encouragement from the General Secretariat to think, explore, experiment, plan, and act on a countrywide basis. Such latitude was notable for having been open to an expatriate, for there were many potential cross-cultural pitfalls during that postindependence transition period. There was pain and joy; there were high points and low points. More than is easily expressed on a personal level, those were fulfilling and enriching years.

II. Program Focus, and Shift toward Rationale and Definition

How to define rural development never presented a serious problem to the NCCK. Needs in Kenya's rural areas seemed as obvious as the commensurate responses. Considered collectively, the projects and activities promoted by the department did not comprise a cohesive predetermined whole. Rationale for action undertaken was rendered fairly straightforward, given that Kenya's economy was based primarily on agriculture, with the majority of its people living in rural areas of the country. Still, the department was selective in its choice of activities. Usually they were characterized by some sense of urgency (drought) or by the sense that certain (semiarid) areas of the country were particularly disadvantaged.

Indeed, if there was any attempt to define rural development, it was in the context of specific issues. The attempt, on occasion, to analyze issues in more detailed fashion took place in specially convened conferences or seminars. But even then, the NCCK contribution tended to focus on the immediate community dynamics of a situation.

There was the latent implication that rural development issues were best resolved if not left entirely in the hands of professionals or of expert technicians. There was the sense that peasant farmers and pastoralists, individually and collectively, were behaving rationally. Properly understood, the rural person and rural communities were to be viewed not as constraints or as problems to be solved. Rural communities were to be understood as both resource and agency under the general rubric of rural development.

Integral to an appreciation of rural peoples was the matter of indigenous knowledge and praxis. Tradition was seen as the Achilles' heel of rural development. It informed most rural relationships, influenced much of national politics, and gave content to and reflected rural wisdom. But in the typical development debate, tradition was readily viewed as constraint rather than as resource. In modest ways, the department sought to foster a more positive view of rural communities and rural traditions.

To summarize, the department's focus was not clear. It was, rather, an uneasy shuffle among a variety of actors—a marriage of convenience with various levels of Kenyan government policy, a determined affirmation of the genius of rural people, and a refusal to settle for easy solutions. It was a less-than-satisfactory attempt to work alongside and together with NCCK member churches. More positively, it was a belief that the earth, properly stewarded, could feed everyone adequately.

III. Northern Kenya

For NCCK purposes, Northern Kenya referred to the administrative districts of Mandera, Marsabit, Turkana, Isiolo, Garissa, and Tana River. More euphemistically, the term referred to Kenya's arid and semiarid areas. The eastern border had long been contentiously disputed with Somalia, while the whole of the north was referred to as the "Northern Frontier District," and was for a long time accessible only with special permission. In the frontier town of Isiolo, a physical barricade on the main road marked the entrance to "Northern Kenya."

Turkana

During colonial times, the north of Kenya was essentially off limits to development activity. The "opening" of the north coincided with droughts and floods to which there was liberal response from the NCCK in the form of famine relief, distributed in several strategically located camps. Homes for orphan children were established, and a village polytechnic, sponsored in part by the NCCK, and an initiative toward the establishment of a fishermen's cooperative on the shore of Lake Turkana at Kalokol were launched. NCCK personnel staffed the relief camps, administered the children's home, and provided a degree of coordination for voluntary agency efforts in the Kalokol area.

During the years under review, the NCCK profile in Turkana changed slightly. When the appointed field officer resigned, much of the coordination for NCCK-funded activity shifted to the resident Africa Inland Church (AIC) missionary, initially an expatriate, later a Kenyan. After some hesitation, the AIC began to take "ownership" of NCCK-funded activity. It was an uneasy relationship, suspended between ready NCCK funding, on the one hand, and some continuing tension between the AIC and the overseas Africa Inland Mission, on the other.

NCCK relationships with the several projects in the area were direct, coordinated in situ by occasional visits. The AIC office in Nairobi was generally not a link within the coordination loop. As a consequence, the NCCK-supported projects in the Kalokol area seemed always to be of mixed parentage, and thus in some measure of uncertain tutelage. Some projects in the area were supported with good funding and strong administrative bases. For example, the Fishermen's Cooperative had become the object of Norwegian aid under the umbrella of Kenya's cooperative movement. The children's home was "owned and operated" by social workers within the

NCCK's Urban Improvement Project. And a community basket-making project was being funded by the NCCK, but destined for "ownership" by the continuing AIC presence.

Like other parts of northern Kenya, Turkana was afflicted by the scourge of insecurity. So-called *ngoroko*—armed cattle rustlers—periodically terrorized Turkana and Pokot communities. *Ngoroko* activity had long plagued the area, but was rendered more deadly with the acquisition of modern automatic weapons. Political instability across the border in Uganda, together with the relatively distant Ogaden conflict in eastern Ethiopia, served as sources of weapons for the *ngoroko* activity.

During a particularly severe spate of *ngoroko* violence, churches and missions active in Turkana and Pokot areas asked NCCK to host a meeting to discuss the problem. Both *ngoroko* violence and the consequent reprisals from the Kenyan government's General Service Unit—seen by some church personnel as unduly severe—were considered in those meetings. In turn, protests from churches were criticized by representatives of the Kenyan government as interference with legitimate, routine security measures.

Even though church protests were not particularly well received by government officers, the forum that birthed them lent itself readily to other purposes. Thus was established the Turkana Churches Coordinating Committee (TCCC), meeting twice a year, focused on an expanding agenda. Typically, the TCCC meetings discussed the coordination of drought-relief activities within the district, together with livestock-improvement proposals and aspects of irrigation development.

The department's role in providing a coordination forum in Turkana represented a substantial NCCK influence in the district. It was assumed in that context that NCCK resources for Turkana would be channeled through its member churches. But there was always a caveat. Like the sands of Turkana, the chemistry of church relations and church activities in the district could and did change at short notice. And with the completion of the Kenya-Sudan highway, passing as it did through Turkana District, it was assumed that the pace of change would quicken.

Marsabit District

Marsabit District was blessed with spectacular natural beauty, varying from its island of forest atop Marsabit Mountain to the craters on the edge of the desert. It was in Marsabit District that NCCK most effectively developed the notion of a "growth center." The needs to which the NCCK responded had been generated by a series of droughts, by *shifta* ("bandit") activity, and by periodic political upheavals in Ethiopia and Somalia. The unease along the borders with Ethiopia, and even with relatively distant Somalia, was fed during those years by disputes between Ethiopia and Somalia regarding ownership of the Ogaden territory in eastern Ethiopia. It was fueled as well by debate within Somalia with regard to the meaning of "Greater Somalia" (areas with a majority Somali population), relevant to border areas of Kenya and Ethiopia. It was fueled, finally, by the collapse in 1974 of the Ethiopian feudal empire and the subsequent ideologically radical political and economic reorientation of that country. Together, those dynamics contributed directly and indirectly to the loss of livestock, to human displacement, and to the need for rehabilitation.

Much NCCK activity focused on agriculture in a cluster of villages along the Ethiopia-Kenya border—namely, Uran, Sololo, Dabalafachana, Moyale, Monsille, Nana, Dodana, Dabel, and Oda. Encircling Mt. Marsabit were the settlements of Songa, Kitruni, Nasikakwe, Badassa, and Bubisa. Agricultural success was most pronounced in Songa, with its reticulated "teaspoon" irrigation system.

Ethiopian refugee farmers at Badassa became self-sufficient in record time, but they had farming in their genes. For purposes of ready self-sufficiency, they required only the most modest access to seeds, tools, and housing. Indeed, their success became something of a tension point in the community.

As a cohesive, long-term community, Uran was probably the most interesting. Dabalafachana suffered from shell shock and an uncertain water supply. Border villages to the east of Moyale had been largely abandoned during the Ogaden War and the related, intense *shifta* activity. Moyale town was under siege at least once during that period, forcing NCCK staff to seek cover under tables and beds. *Shifta* attacks on vehicles traveling the Great North Road were often fatal. Fortunately, NCCK staff were spared.

Agriculturally, the border settlements enjoyed only modest, sporadic success. Dabel seemed to be located in a rain shadow, with water supply a constant problem. In this regard, its situation was similar to conditions prevailing in Nasikakwe on the southern slopes of Mt. Marsabit. However, some positive results were in evidence. For many pastoralists, the settlements provided "breathing space." They served as sources of food for semi-settled families and as sources of occasional earnings from the sale of cash crops while every effort was made to rebuild livestock holdings. For children, the settlements provided an exposure to formal education—for the first time, in many cases. For government officers, the settlements provided access to people who were otherwise on the move. For NCCK staff, it provided opportunity to test cash crops, food crops, and tree varieties. Settlements provided church personnel with opportunities to serve and to share. Throughout, NCCK field staff undertook myriad roles, experimenting, liaising, transporting, instructing, repairing, supplying, and servicing all manner of processes and relationships among these semi-pastoral people. They performed in the most remarkable manner under seemingly impossible conditions.

Generally, the settlements were viewed as development symbols bringing semi-pastoral peoples into the mainstream of national life. In fact, they served as access points to an enlarged risk base. Pastoralist peoples were fully aware of the need for the broadest possible range of options and relationships. Settlement was one of those options. Some family members were accommodated in the settlements, while others moved about with the remaining livestock. The pastoralists always maintained healthy relationships with their respective extended family members, strategically placed as investments in economic and social security.

The chief weakness in NCCK's Marsabit Program was that, while it acknowledged the inherent livestock expertise of the pastoralist, it did not sufficiently support it. Any viable future for Marsabit District was dependent on careful attention to livestock improvement simply because most of the district was suited primarily to livestock grazing.

In Marsabit District, more than in Turkana District, old rivalries between the churches had long been active. These were, in part, hangovers from the pioneer days of the mission era, when operational territories were delineated according to the dynamics of comity—the association of agencies to mutual benefit—and in other respects the rivalries stemmed from substantive differences in operational modes and approaches. The NCCK presence mitigated the inherent tensions, if only to a degree.

It was NCCK practice to work closely with its member churches in the area, with special regard for the conspicuous presence of the Anglican Church and the Africa Inland Church. Whenever opportunity afforded, there was cooperation with the Catholic Diocese of Marsabit and with related agencies, such as the Catholic Relief Services. In this regard, the Marsabit Churches Development Committee (MCDC), established at some point along the way at NCCK initiative, proved most helpful.

The MCDC was chaired by the Kenyan government's resident district commissioner. Local elders, as well as representatives from all church groups active in the district, were invited to attend the periodic meetings. Government officers from various departments attended the meetings, as did representatives from secular development agencies. For NCCK purposes, the committee provided a public forum in which ongoing NCCK projects could be reviewed, where innovations were tested, and where plans for new projects were announced. It provided a forum where the NCCK could be publicly accountable and a means by which to invite member churches and fraternal agencies to do the same. It provided opportunity to record in public the intent of a given agency to undertake a given project. After announcement in this forum, such plans usually found their way to the District Development Committee, a formal government-sponsored forum, for final approval. One of the projects that surfaced repeatedly for discussion in the MCDC was the Huri Hills Project.

The Huri Hills comprise a plateau area—thirty by ninety kilometers—northwest of Marsabit Mountain. Development activity for this dry-season grazing resource was proposed originally by an AIC missionary. It was an unusual project because it claimed to have given due consideration to ecological concerns. In the event, the project design was assisted by the UN's ecology team based at Mt. Kulal and by the NCCK's forester-ecologist.

The Huri Hills Project fell outside the normal NCCK administrative structure. It was seen, essentially, as an Africa Inland Mission/Africa Inland

Church project benefiting from certain NCCK support services such as initial reconnaissance, evaluation, and liaison with the donor. In a second phase of the project, the donor arranged for direct relationship with the AIC, which in turn established its own committee supervision for the project. Committee membership included an NCCK staff person, facilitating a way for the NCCK to relate to the implementation phase of the project.

In Marsabit District, the NCCK presence was many-sided. On the one hand were the operational projects, with NCCK staff performing actual field tasks; on the other were the relationship-monitoring dynamics vis-à-vis churches active in the district and the Kenyan government. There were some successes: trees were planted and thrived, hot chilies found a market, relief food became food-for-work, settlements developed into communities. But the successes called for assessment in light of the enormity of the district and in light of an extraordinarily fragile ecology. Just below the surface of department activity was a nagging suspicion that far too little was known and appreciated about pastoralists. There was the concomitant sense that the best-planned development project could be shriveled into nothing by a severe drought, by border politics, and by the sheer distance from modern-sector supply and communication centers.

Particularly symbolic of the tenuous links with down-country Kenya were the department's efforts in water development. The district water officer repeatedly reminded NCCK staff that at any one time the mechanical pumps on more than half of the wells in the district were dysfunctional. Maintenance was poor, diesel oil was missing, a spare part was not available…as though a conspiracy against modern mechanical systems was in effect. Two water installations, to which the NCCK contributed, deserve comment.

Uran village featured a well-designed water-pumping system. It was equipped with a diesel-powered generator supporting a submersible electric pump. Several local men had been trained for its maintenance, while the water reticulation system had been built with strong harambee (local volunteer) support. Eventually, the pumping station had been handed over to the Kenyan government for its continuing operation and the requisite maintenance. It functioned reasonably well, but not optimally. However, compared to other water projects, it was the tidiest mechanical water development contribution initiated by the NCCK.

At the other end of the spectrum was the mechanical water system in Dabel village. Originally a joint Catholic-NCCK project, it eventually fell into disrepair. Meanwhile, the local religious guru had had a dream about an alternative well site. Through his guidance, the community was motivated to dig a new well by hand. Thus was a water source successfully identified. Water was drawn from the well by an indigenous bucket-and-rope system, defying mechanical breakdowns.

Water sources in Marsabit District were not abundant and did not lend themselves readily to modern extraction and storage systems. The ecologist standing by would nod approvingly, aware that easy access to water in a semiarid zone could in the long run prove not to be a blessing.

As in Turkana, there was increasing evidence that the development role of NCCK member churches in Marsabit District was growing. The department took some satisfaction in having facilitated such participation. Along the way, government officers endorsed various NCCK initiatives, always ready to show visitors the Songa settlement scheme as an example of development. At one point, the department actively explored ways of stimulating improvements within the existing livestock infrastructure. One small step in that direction took the form of sending select candidates from the district to the one-year ranching course offered by the Isinya Rural Center in Maasailand, some distance south of Nairobi. It was, finally, most satisfying to observe the effective participation of local people in the change process. Given opportunity, people make appropriate choices during an evolving transition period.

Isiolo District

Isiolo District served as the doorkeeper to northern Kenya. That role was symbolized by a road barrier on the northern edge of Isiolo town and by the required registration of all travelers to the north. If the barrier did not by itself maintain the peace, it did alert the traveler that the area remained vulnerable to *shifta* activity. Such activity had disrupted the smooth operation of the NCCK's Rapsu Irrigation Scheme by drawing attention to the ethnic composition of the scheme's membership. Along the way, the expatriate scheme manager had been forced to leave, a sacrifice to the disturbances.

A relative lull in *shifta* activity coincided with a rather important shift in the profile of the Rapsu Irrigation Scheme. Upon careful examination, the scheme was found to have been overcapitalized, and it had been established with a structure requiring high levels of management.

Like other irrigation schemes in the dry zones, it had been established on the assumption that scheme members would make a commitment to permanent settlement. And indeed, some members did exactly that. But others left in the wake of *shifta* disturbances, while the dedicated keepers of animals left when they had accumulated money sufficient to reestablish their herds. As a general practice, the settlers made the choice of keeping some family members in a settlement scheme while others were off with the herds. At work was the age-old pattern of spreading risk.

As noted, tension points in NCCK's Isiolo projects centered on politics related to the activities of the *shifta*. Among district officers, there was vigorous discussion regarding acceptable technical and management levels in the irrigation schemes. The Kinna Irrigation Scheme, initiated by the NCCK, was viewed by the officers as having been neglected. In fact, it seemed that the scheme's management style was merely reflecting accommodation to an indigenously appropriate leadership pattern. And while the scheme was not optimally productive, it did produce astonishing quantities of bananas and other food crops. In a unique way, it had become indigenized in its service to the Kinna community.

A similar debate was generated with regard to the Bulessa Irrigation Scheme. Experts insisted that soils on the scheme were too saline for effective agriculture. And the bits of good soil within the scheme area were considered too limited to warrant assistance toward an organized permanent settlement. NCCK staff ignored expert advice and the "big" expectations of district officers, responding instead to the specific requests for aid from people living and working on the Bulessa Scheme.

Ensuing results seemed to justify the NCCK's response. The level of motivation and participation among scheme members proved to be exceptionally high. Scheme members had time to tend small livestock feeding on nearby bushes that had deliberately been left uncleared. The Bulessa Scheme seemed to demonstrate that small was manageable, even beautiful.

On the macro level, the NCCK presence in Isiolo District had been coordinated for the most part through the official District Development Committee. But members of the respective irrigation schemes had selected their own representative management or coordinating committees. Because of *shifta* tensions, the Rapsu Scheme Committee was elected under the supervision of the district officer. It was an exercise superbly carried out, successfully accommodating the disparate ethnic loyalties in the scheme.

Over time, NCCK activity in the district had adjusted to an uneasy accommodation with *shifta* politics. At the same time, ongoing discussions regarding viability levels for small-scale irrigation continued indefinitely.

Tana River District

For more than one hundred years, villages along the lower Tana River had been influenced by Christian mission activity. As a result, much of the community initiative for so-called development or modernization emanated from the churches, in considerable contrast to other northern districts in which leadership was exercised in a more traditional mode.

During the early 1970s, church-oriented groups along the river had repeatedly requested NCCK assistance. Possibilities related to modern irrigation had already tweaked their imaginations. A series of visits by NCCK staff were made, resulting eventually in the formation of the Tana River Church Coordinating Committee (TRCCC). Its establishment was slow and tedious, taking into account long-established rivalries, and denominational and personality differences.

Once organized, the TRCCC presented NCCK with a request for assistance with irrigation improvement and development. In turn, NCCK sought expert assistance from ecumenical donor agencies in the Netherlands. Within a remarkably short time, two couples with multiple skills were recruited. Their arrival coincided with the establishment of the Small-Scale Irrigation Unit (SSIU) in the Ministry of Agriculture.

After careful consultation between NCCK staff and the SSIU, it was agreed that the latter would adopt the Lower Tana basin as an area of priority for project activity. This because NCCK field staff were already on the ground, and were prepared to assist in data collection and planning. But it was also agreed upon because the government felt that planning for irrigation in the Lower Tana basin should be undertaken within a single coordinated administrative structure. So, for the NCCK, it was a choice of working within the SSIU context, thus facilitating an area plan, or going it alone with one or two villages. In the end, the decision was made to work in cooperation with the SSIU. On the local level, this called for collaboration within the structure of the Provincial Irrigation Unit.

The agreed mandate for the NCCK team was to "humanize" the irrigation development, or, in some cases, the irrigation rehabilitation process. As in any such coordinated effort, perceptions of what should be undertaken varied. Work plans were constantly rescheduled and the red tape of government bureaucracy was frustrating. Tensions between the ideal and the possible, between planning patterns and farmer needs, between peasant and expert were ever apparent. After four years of fieldwork, the findings of an evaluation exercise were instructive. It became clear that everyone involved had entertained unrealistically high hopes with regard to the implementation schedule.

The irrigation engineer on the NCCK team had spent much of his time on data collection and administration, initially, of the Provincial Irrigation Unit's infrastructure. It was a thankless job well done. Meanwhile, the agronomist on the team painstakingly reconstructed the history of local rice varieties. From these, he devised planning modules that could be slotted into the macro-irrigation plan for the Lower Tana basin. It proved to be a satisfying achievement, a fulfilment of the NCCK's "humanizing" mandate.

One member of the team developed a women's work program, which was adopted by the national YMCA. Another made efforts to establish pro forma patterns of village-administered primary health care. As government policy on primary health care was less than fully established, this sector of the team's work did not find a readily structured "home" during the initial project period.

In retrospect, the Lower Tana Village Irrigation Project was complex. Seemingly endless hours were invested in positioning the contribution of the NCCK team. All along, the team was imbued with high levels of creativity, expectation, and motivation. Indeed, their persistence amid formidable odds was remarkable. But in the final analysis, it became clear that the best intentions and the most strenuous efforts must ultimately be fitted into the pace of change determined by many more interests and forces than could readily be managed, even by most dedicated expatriate experts.

Although the original request for assistance had been formulated by the local church committee, it became obvious over time that only certain aspects of the team's work were in fact understood by the church or village groups. Modern irrigation planning proved to be a complex process. In retrospect, it had become clear that the team should have included an interpreter, distilling the intricacies of the process into a more understandable local happening. Such an interpreter/educator/liaison team member was envisioned for the subsequent phase of the project. The NCCK's humanizing role in the Lower Tana region seemed to have been particularly apt. It was a contribution left to ferment within the larger change process in the hope that the whole of the small-scale irrigation plan and its implementation would in fact become more palatable to the smallholder farmers in the Lower Tana River region.

Mandera District

NCCK had moved into Mandera District guided, in part, by a Quaker vision. In the early 1970s, British Quakers had taken the first steps toward the establishment of a "peace presence" in the Horn of Africa. At the time, a Quaker volunteer was on site in the Ogaden region of Ethiopia. Later, it was envisioned, there would be further placement of personnel in both Kenya and Somalia.

In 1974, the Friends (Quakers) of London commissioned a preliminary survey of Mandera District with a view toward the establishment of a service presence at an appropriate site. By 1976, an Australian couple recruited by London Friends was in Kenya, with a commitment to placement in Rhamu, a small village fifty miles west of Mandera town.

During the two years prior to the opening of the center, much effort had been invested in negotiating a workable Quaker-NCCK relationship. Numerous visits with the district commissioner in Mandera, with government officers, and with community leaders in Rhamu village were made. Adding spice to the mix were three Italian volunteers nearing the end of their service period with the Mandera Boys Center and now scouting about for another service engagement. As they were onsite, ready for action, and more or less knowledgeable about the area, they were taken on as an advance NCCK staff team for the Rhamu center.

Those volunteers must take much of the credit for organizing the first project of the Center—the construction of staff housing. It was an exercise in simplicity, constructed with local materials, built by local skilled workers, and supervised by a local Rhamu spokesperson. Everything about the arrangements worked superbly well. Completion of construction was accomplished as per the contract. A small postconstruction gratuity was paid to workmen, a sop to the monetary inflation that was supposedly doing its work in this remote place. By any standards, it was a modest cost overrun.

Houses of similar design soon began taking shape throughout the village: at the Harambee Secondary School, at the Ministry of Works compound, and at the local Health Center. They were cool and comfortable—in contrast to the modern style of the district officer's house. Appreciated as appropriate development symbols, the buildings were in every way an affirmation of local resources as the initial statement of the NCCK presence and as an appropriate setting of the mood for subsequent services offered by the center.

During the center's gestation period, numerous discussions with village leaders had led to requests for assistance: NCCK should bring tractors, give loans, build a hospital, and operate a proper irrigation scheme—these among others comprised an extensive wish list. From the NCCK staff, the response was always the same: "Our capacity is modest, funds are limited, and we make no promises. Let our staff live with you and discuss with you. Together, the appropriate initiatives will be identified and undertaken." Such were the disclaimers, repeated on several occasions.

After a four-year NCCK presence, the achievements had little resemblance to the earlier requests. The village was full of neem trees, and kitchen gardens were studded with papaya and guava trees. The long-dormant Rhamu Farmers Cooperative Society was newly reregistered and functioning, thanks to the persistence of a center staff member. The society was managing several irrigation pumps, including a partially successful version of a solar-powered submersible electric pump. Village initiative had engaged with the NCCK tree nursery for planting a community woodlot, and the beginnings of a primary health service were taking shape.

The Rhamu Service Center was birthed by a vision of peace in the Horn of Africa. That vision informed the choice of personnel for the center as well as the nature of the activities promoted. It was to this end that NCCK Rhamu staff invested much time and effort in forming relationships with the local Muslim sheikh whose followers were found in this tri-corner region of Kenya, Ethiopia, and Somalia. In commensurate ways, the staff at the center were expected to think beyond the restrictions imposed by the respective national borders.

Irrigation

Together with other villages along the Daua River (marking the border between Kenya and Ethiopia), Rhamu was deemed to have irrigation potential; in fact, for years basic irrigation had been carried out along the river. The unstable border situation had kept major irrigation schemes from being implemented. FAO's Border Post One Scheme, located just on the perimeter of Mandera town was the exception. Given the ambiguities of the small- and medium-scale irrigation experience in Kenya, it was in retrospect fortuitous that the NCCK was not committed to any large-scale irrigation assistance on the Daua River.

NCCK's sojourn with irrigation development had all along been rather uneasy. There was the tension between capital-intensive and low-cost schemes, and between the demands of pastoral life and the technical expertise required of irrigated farming, in addition to many other considerations. In an effort to package irrigation experience to date, the department convened a conference in April 1981 focusing on the issues related to small-scale irrigation.

Conference agenda featured discussion on small-scale irrigation, on optimal relationships with livestock and forage components, and on ways of maximizing traditional indigenous knowledge. Conference findings seemed to suggest that small-scale irrigation, carefully adjusted to reflect local ecological and traditional farmer needs, held some promise for modestly successful implementation.

Livestock

As noted above, concern with livestock development had not featured prominently in NCCK's northern Kenya programs. As a program focus, agriculture was better organized. But the livestock program deficiency was, in some measure, recognized. In 1980, a preliminary survey was commissioned by the department, seeking to identify ways of enlarging support for livestock development. Earlier government plans for enormous block ranches had meanwhile been abandoned. Those plans were on a scale that effectively excluded nongovernmental agencies (including church agencies) from any meaningful role. After those plans were scuttled, it seemed in order for the quest by a voluntary agency to seek out an appropriate initiative for livestock improvement.

IV. Institutions

Rural Training Centers

In the early 1960s, the NCCK had received 400,000 British pounds from Christian Aid UK to establish six Rural Training Centers (RTCs). These were intended to offer training to facilitate the smooth transfer of former European farmland to Kenyan smallholder farmers. It was a major exercise, addressing the country's most contested issue, land. It was an initiative very much at the heart of tensions and unrealized promise in postindependence Kenya. The NCCK-sponsored RTCs were intended to function as a mediating dynamic during those transition years.

Supervisory administration of the centers was coordinated by the department's major committee, known at the time as the Relief, Rehabilitation and Rural Development Committee ("3Rs"). This committee periodically convened administrators from the respective centers—each affiliated with a respective NCCK member church—and representatives from relevant government ministries for purposes of coordination.

It was an effective arrangement until the overseas donors sent a signal to the effect that the NCCK would need to identify ways of generating local support for the RTCs. That signal was the beginning of protracted negotiations with both government ministries and with the relevant member churches in a process that stretched into years and produced, finally, a variety of local support models.

Eventually, one of the RTCs came under the effective administration of the sponsoring church, and another center was farmed out to a training program for overseas volunteers while internal problems of the sponsoring church were being resolved. Administrative responsibility for yet another center was taken over completely by the Kenyan government. A fourth center became engaged in the throes of untangling an existing government–NCCK–church–sponsored administrative arrangement, with the church sponsor eventually accepting a larger administrative role. The RTC training complex in Masaailand forged ahead with a strong management committee, but at the same time struggled financially to keep its extensive institutional structure of subcenters functioning, as the latter were spread over a huge geographical area. Finally, a small center on the semiarid eastern slopes of Mt. Kenya was integrated into a district-level regional livestock-improvement program, sponsored by the UK government in collaboration with the Kenyan government.

Generation of local support for the RTCs was much more complex than indicated by the above summary. But the arrangements that were eventually settled upon constituted a reasonably satisfactory shift from dependence on overseas donors to local support. Dynamics of the exercise had made it clear that institutions of this kind have a stubborn will to live. Even when they operate suboptimally, they meet select needs: prestige needs, employment needs, and the need for general institutional reference points, obviously committed to some semblance of a change or modern-sector process.

On the other hand, there were certain inherent negative characteristics related to RTCs. Vigilant management demands competed with the need for creative innovation and the perennial search for adequate funds. Within an institutional context, it was of course easier to merely "tick over." Such were the problem dynamics plaguing all the RTCs. Transfer to total government management did not solve the problem. Indeed, some of the problems were at times exacerbated by the transition process. In at least some of the communities surrounding the RTCs, farmers were operating more effectively than were the supposedly exemplary RTCs. Measured in those terms, the six RTCs had performed only moderately well. There was some consolation in the realization that government-sponsored RTCs generally functioned no better.

With the benefit of hindsight, much would have been gained by an earlier NCCK withdrawal from the coordination role. Typically, agenda related to the RTCs dominated the 3Rs meetings and in the process functioned as opportunity costs. Coinciding with the transition of NCCK-related RTCs to local support was government-sponsored research on the most efficacious means of stimulating rural development in independent Kenya. Among the more striking findings was evidence that small-scale farmers learned more from their small-scale neighbor farmers with regard to agricultural innovations than they did from either government or church-sponsored RTCs. According to word-of-mouth reports, the weeklong courses at RTCs were viewed by some farmers as vacation time rather than learning time. Other reports indicated that during the transition from large-scale European settler farms to indigenous smallholder farms, the gross agricultural product rose significantly; according to one finding, by as much as five-fold! Was small-scale intensive (backbreaking with a hoe) farming inherently more productive than large-scale (machinery-assisted) extensive farming? Did RTCs provide any positive stimulus to that increased production? These critical queries were noted but not scrutinized in sufficient detail to be of utility to the NCCK experience.

Village Polytechnics

When the first draft of this reflection was begun in 1981, Kenya featured over three hundred village polytechnics (VPs), thanks in large measure to NCCK initiative. It was an initiative birthed during the 1960s in response to the vocational training needs of primary school leavers. NCCK's role in the development of VPs was that of initial prime mover, as instigator of trial-and-error exercises, and eventually as promoter of functioning models.

VPs developed into a national movement. In 1973, a formal ceremony marked the shift of the VP program from the NCCK to Kenyan government administration, which shouldered the overall planning, coordination, and implementation responsibility for VPs, while the NCCK continued in an auxiliary role as grass-roots stimulator—especially among constituent member churches—and as a supplementary source of funds and ideas. On the basis of numerous evaluations, there was no doubt that VPs met a real need. Thousands of youngsters acquired skills and jobs because of the VP movement.

In many ways, the VP experience demonstrated nongovernmental agency (NGO) action at its best: as stimulant, catalyst, and innovator. The handover exercise posed the question whether an NGO such as the NCCK should give priority to further institution-building or whether its initiatives should shift in other directions. In general, Kenya was reasonably well served with an institutional infrastructure, but always in a quest to close the gap between routine management, on the one hand, and best practices, on the other. Obviously, "best practices" called for a constant flow of ideas, innovations, and suggestions. Given a substantial choice, the NGO would probably have done best to let management find its own way—all kinds of specialized management courses by technical institutes were on offer—and to concentrate on generating and sharing cutting-edge ideas with existing institutions. It was a point of continuing discussion.

V. Rural Energy

Animal Traction

Already in the early 1970s, it became clear that all was not well on the rural energy scene. Constraints and frustrations appeared most dramatically among Kenya's farmers, who since shortly after independence had occupied the former "White Highlands." Many farmers could not afford to buy tractors. In some cases, farmers could not effectively operate tractors already in their possession because of high-cost fuel and spare parts. Meanwhile, the existing tractor hire services on offer by the Kenya government were unable to meet the needs of those who owned neither tractors nor oxen.

Teaming up with the Faculty of Agriculture and the Institute of Development Studies, both ensconced within the University of Nairobi, the department organized a major conference in August 1975 focused on animal traction.

The conference featured much of the current knowledge regarding the comparative advantages of using tractors versus oxen versus human labor in farming operations. A report on the conference, produced by the Institute of Development Studies, was identified as Occasional Paper No. 16 of August 1975. The document eventually found its way into the planning division of the Ministry of Agriculture, where it provided basic data for an FAO animal-traction project, which was under consideration at the time. After much revision and discussion, the FAO project got underway. As the project had been born in the wake of the 1975 conference, it followed that the department continued to associate with the project in a monitoring mode.

Specifically, the department acted as secretary to a committee that had undertaken the planning for the 1975 conference and that for the subsequent five years provided the context for the development of the FAO project. Meanwhile, the FAO project matured, monitoring field tests of animal-drawn equipment that had been manufactured as prototypes.

Already during the field trial stage of the project, serious constraints became evident. Access to sufficient quantities of uniform-quality steel was not assured. Nor was it clear that the manufacturing capability of Kenyan industry could meet the standards of either the quality or quantity required by the project.

The whole exercise was useful as a test of the value of the catalytic action by an NGO, bringing together the academic community (university), an international agency (FAO), a government ministry (agriculture), and various other NGOs. During this period, church-related animal-traction projects provided training in ox-guidance systems. Those programs trained a large number of Kenya government officers, and in fact established the norms for the country's formal ox-use systems.

Subsequently, fuel prices increased substantially and the need for alternative energy sources became more urgent. The implementation stage of the project coincided with the launch of a national food policy paper in the form of Sessional Paper No. 4 of 1981, which identified the animal-traction project as a component of the country's food-production strategy. The six-year odyssey in search of better deployment of animal power had reached an important juncture.

Windmills

For many years, windmills had been successfully deployed by European ranchers on the Laikipia Plains of Kenya. But at some point, the local agent decided that the sale of diesel-powered pumps was more lucrative than the sale of windmills. As a consequence, windmill use declined.

In the face of the rising energy costs, various groups became interested in windmills, both in terms of general promotion and in-country manufacture. An engineer at the University of Nairobi built a number of prototypes that were tested at various sites. At some point in that process, the NCCK became involved with the funding of these experimental windmills. It was eventually agreed that a windmill-manufacturing unit would be established within the Nairobi Christian Industrial Training Center (CITC). An expert windmill engineer became available and a supervisory committee was established.

The windmill project was one effort that failed in virtually all respects. Technical designs were controversial and the workshop was not properly equipped or staffed. Nor were there qualified personnel to undertake the necessary field testing, design alteration, sales promotion, and training. It was a case of trying to do too much in the context of serious constraints in every aspect of the undertaking. Eventually, the whole effort was disbanded. Subsequently, the CITC manufactured an occasional windmill following a specific request from some buyer. High marks must be given to the CITC staff for even attempting what became an unwieldy project.

Apart from the CITC project, the 3Rs Department monitored and supported other windmill-promotion efforts. One of these took the form of a written survey of existing windmill use, research, and manufacture. It enjoyed wide circulation, providing data for other research projects.

Meanwhile, the manufacture of commercial windmills did in fact become established in Kenya. In addition, several feasibility studies examining windmill potential in Kenya were published. The 3Rs Department slowly withdrew from the windmill-promotion effort, partly to lick its wounds, and partly because active interest in windmills had meanwhile gained momentum, both in the commercial sector and in the Ministry of Energy's policy process. There remained the challenge of integrating windmill technology with irrigation systems, with small-scale farming systems, and with the training and extension facilities of the Ministry of Water Development.

Biogas

Biogas is a natural gas produced by anaerobic bacteria active in the fermentation of animal dung or other biomass. The gas can be used for cooking, lighting, and power generation. Both diesel- and petrol-powered engines can be adapted to operate on biogas. An additional advantage accruing from biogas production has to do with the "spent slurry" or post-fermentation residue, which is an effective fertilizer.

For more than twenty-five years, a European farmer in Kenya had been generating and using biogas and the ensuing slurry. He was invited on occasion to share his experience and expertise with members of the NCCK's 3Rs committee, which he did, though cautiously and reluctantly. He expressed some fear that the biogas equipment that he had designed might be replicated without proper permission. In the absence of meaningful collaboration with him, the department mounted its own modest information-gathering and -sharing exercise.

A British biogas engineer was employed on a part-time basis to prepare an inventory on the status of biogas use, research, and potential in Kenya. Several reports were prepared, some of which were submitted for discussion to a national Biogas Conference convened at Egerton College, sponsored by the British Council, where it attracted keen interest.

The conference coincided with preparations for a National Energy Symposium—an event that eventually contributed to the establishment of the Ministry of Energy. Various proposals for a national biogas program were entertained subsequently by the Ministry of Energy, informed in some measure by reports prepared by the 3Rs Department. Subsequently, various versions of those proposals were being "bought" by funding agencies or by governments of donor countries.

In addition, small-scale biogas-manufacturing efforts were launched. These held some promise as an immediate response to rocketing fuel-wood costs and declining supplies of kerosene. In the event, interest in biogas as an alternative source of energy for cooking, lighting, engine fuel, and agricultural fertilizer did in fact expand, eventually offering well-designed equipment that became commercially available.

The NCCK role in biogas development was peripheral. Biogas development, like windmill development, required a considerable array of supporting research, testing, and promotion. Factors to be considered included digester design, feeding routines, availability of lamps and cookers, manufacture, training, and farmer education, all requiring single-minded pursuit. As a package, the effort was more than the department could effectively muster. But there was satisfaction in having popularized the potential of biogas in general, and in following up on a number of research elements.

While most of the department's work in biogas promotion was on an ad hoc basis, some aspects found a home in the Rural Development Technology Committee, hosted by the Ministry of Agriculture, which had monitored the animal-traction project. During the course of its rather precarious life (1974–1981), the committee moved from its early ad hoc status to a more or less bona fide permanent entity. It had lived with various designations along the way and had kept a development conversation going among disparate activists.

Forestry

Studies undertaken by means of satellite surveys indicated that the forest-land in Kenya had shrunk from 3.5 percent to 2.5 percent of the total land area from 1975 to 1979. Depletion of forests coincided with the rapid rise of oil prices. In Kenya, where some 95 percent of rural cooking was dependent on firewood, the implications were obvious. The concern for shrinking fuel supplies was voiced by many agencies.

Through Lutheran World Relief (USA), a Canadian forester-ecologist was recruited by the department. He was given the mandate to promote and encourage tree planting by all appropriate means. For these purposes, he was mandated to liaise and engage with churches, with relevant departments in the Kenyan government, and with the appropriate international agencies.

The basic strategy was straightforward. A meeting of interested persons was called to confer on specific needs, on the available resources, and on the priority action to be undertaken. A second step involved the identification of some twenty-three species suitable for planting in Kenya's semiarid areas. Together with this list, there was a compilation of information on germination sequences as well as information regarding the multiple uses of particular species.

The third step involved dissemination of tree seeds to interested persons and church-related organizations. Available seeds were accompanied by report forms to be completed and returned to the NCCK forester-ecologist. In the event, none of the recipients reported on progress made, though rumors suggested that trees were being planted.

At the end of the project's initial three years, a major conference was convened, bringing together interested persons, particularly those who had received seeds earlier on. Conference participants reported informally on their numerous tree planting efforts. In addition to an estimated 250,000 trees planted as a direct result of the department's initiative, it was found that many church-related rural programs were now including tree-planting components in a variety of rural focus projects. Enthusiasm among church groups for tree planting had in fact been stimulated, but largely on an informal basis.

Most of the tree-planting initiative was left to local groups, who devised and followed varying planting procedures. The NCCK provided information on suitable species, seed sources, simple planting techniques, and some sharing of practical information generated by tree-planting enthusiasts.

While much useful information became available from international groups, notably from the Nairobi-based International Council for Research on Agro-Forestry, the project was unsuccessful in stimulating formal coordination of tree-planting efforts on a national scale. Several committees expressed the intention to meet, but that did not happen during the project period.

Project experience would indicate that churches and voluntary agencies in Kenya could mobilize substantial action at grassroots levels. Farmers were definitely interested in planting trees, but lacked advice with regard to appropriate species and were rarely encouraged by the Forest Department to plant indigenous trees. Meanwhile, a sister agency encouraged organized community groups to compile extensive lists of indigenous trees, identifying vernacular names and indicating their indigenous uses. This aspect of the tree-planting effort merited follow-up. It had become evident that in the rush to embrace exotic, fast-growing trees—as promoted by the Ministry of Forestry at the time—much traditional, local wisdom had been neglected.

Of all the projects or initiatives fostered by the department, this one was in many ways the most heartwarming. Response was enthusiastic, and results were in some cases dramatic. After three years, many of the trees were already bearing fruit. Germination knowledge was readily acquired and spread easily from one group to the next.

The little village of Rhamu in northern Kenya was the site of one of the department's tree-planting efforts. To walk into the courtyard of a village homestead under Rhamu's blazing sun and observe a mother and child sitting in the shade of a tree planted at the initiative of the department was more than sufficient reward for the efforts expended in the three-year project.

VI. Inter-Church Rural Development

Generally, the department did poorly in maintaining ties with counterpart programs sponsored by member churches. One rather fruitful exception was in Kitui and Machakos districts.

During the major drought of the mid-1970s, there was a distress call from the churches in these two districts. Churches in Kitui District spoke with a united voice—already nine years earlier they had established a district-level ecumenical committee. During the drought period, it served as a base for coordinating available relief supplies and for subsequent rehabilitation work. In Machakos District, NCCK member churches were less well organized. Indeed, during the height of the drought, NCCK working relations were strongest with the well-organized Catholic Diocese of Machakos.

After an initial period of basic relief activity, the department, together with counterparts in the Catholic Secretariat and the Salvation Army headquarters, prepared a joint seed multiplication project. In both districts, small church-related groups were mobilized to grow and multiply seeds of the traditional drought-resistant food crops—millets, sorghums, chickpeas, and cowpeas.

It was a rather frantic effort because some communities had in fact neglected those traditional, more or less drought-resistant crops in favor of short-season maize recently developed by the nearby research station. The maize had done well upon its introduction some ten years earlier, as its initial availability had coincided with several years of good rains. When the more or less normal drought cycle reemerged, there was insufficient rain for the maize, while seeds for the drought-resistant crops were simply not available in sufficient quantities.

Following the first harvest of the "seed multiplying" exercise, seminars for farmers and church and community leaders were convened. It was an attempt to rejuvenate drought-resistant crops, a process greatly facilitated by a timely policy switch in the Kenyan government that strongly encouraged the growing of diversified drought-resistant food crops, including those featured in the NCCK "bulking" project.

At about this point, there was a sense in the department that more effort needed to be devoted to the organization of NCCK member churches for long-term rehabilitation of the area. In future, droughts would no doubt recur, but their effects could, with appropriate action, be mitigated.

Thus began a protracted exercise in discussing, evaluating, and restructuring. Out of this effort emerged a properly constituted NCCK "branch" in Kitui District with its own rural development committee. In Machakos District, a proper NCCK "branch" was slow to be organized but an ecumenically based rural development committee was firmly established.

The restructuring process was greatly enhanced by the appointment of an NCCK field officer in Machakos District. It was his responsibility to coordinate all aspects of the department's presence and assistance in the two districts. In a short time, the field officer was fully occupied in monitoring committee meetings, organizing seminars, and, in Machakos District, co-coordinating projects on site. In both districts, he spent much time liaising with government officers and with Catholic counterparts.

The work in Kitui District was guided on a day-to-day basis by an officer seconded from the Ministry of Agriculture to supervise the field work of both the NCCK Kitui branch and the Catholic Diocese of Kitui. Coordination of this rather ungainly relationship was accomplished to everyone's satisfaction.

Eventually, the program in the two districts helped to raise the level of awareness in churches, particularly on issues such as the stewardship of the land. The several seminars were followed by short two-day training programs in which practical skills were demonstrated and shared.

Such skills included the construction of small water-storage tanks, the construction of spring covers and subsurface or sand dams, and the construction of bench terraces. Some of these skills were shared by NCCK employees. In other cases, skilled persons from elsewhere were identified and made available to organized groups for mini training courses. In subsequent years, sand dams became a major focus, with many hundreds constructed by community groups in Kitui and Machakos districts.

Thus the role of the NCCK's field officer for the two districts was that of overall coordination with government officers, churches, committees, community work groups, and with other formal development efforts such as the Catholic Christian Development Education Services and the government-related Machakos Integrated Development Program.

This program easily ranked as the department's most rewarding interaction with a community of churches, committed to both theological reflection and practical rural action. It could not be cited as an unmitigated success nor as a ready model to be replicated in other areas. But in this case, the arrangement worked well. Of special note were the following:

- The shift from relief to remedial development activity.

- The joint engagement with Catholics, government officers, and various other agencies.
- The move from ad hoc liaising structures to established committees.
- The combined emphasis on theory and practice.
- The multiplication and sharing of skills.
- The emphasis on the catalytic role of the NCCK rather than an ever-growing administrative structure.
- The emphasis on a recycling of indigenous knowledge regarding food, trees, and grasses.

VII. Issues in Rural Development

The much lauded and widely promoted First (1960s) and Second (1970s) Development Decades as declared by the United Nations provided much of the ethos in the post–World War II period, leading into the postcolonial (politically independent) period in Africa. Between 1972 and 1982, the United Nations convened eighteen global conferences on a broad range of issues, including water, food, health, and the environment. Those conferences identified acceptable or preferred standards of living for people in UN member states. As might have been expected, those identified standards were hugely informed by prevailing living standards in Western countries. In some sense, "development" undertakings constituted the Westernization of non-Western countries.

A Theology for (Rural) Development

The change or development tools deployed by African churches and NGOs in the immediate postindependence period were forged, in significant measure, in secular, modern Western foundries. They did not emerge from the life of the African church. The available change tools generally bespoke efficiencies, foreign technologies, and capital-intensive ventures. Indigenous praxis and indigenous people were too readily viewed by the development process as problems to be solved.

Those characteristics of the modern development process were particularly stark when compared to the biblical position that all people were created in and reflective of the image of God. Furthermore, the Bible seemed to offer clear guidelines for the change sojourn of the people of God.

In the Old Testament, that sojourn was toward and with the "Promised Land." The development and growth of peoplehood was closely identified with proper stewardship of the land. One of the striking paradigms bringing "people" and "land" together is found in the "Jubilee" (Lev. 25), suggesting Shalom or a model of "right relationships" for the development sojourn. The New Testament continues with "Jubilary" themes (Luke 4:16-18), and of course the ministry of Jesus Christ demonstrated radical concern for the poor and for justice.

Land as place and as promise lies at the heart of the Jubilee model, and thus at the center of all meaningful social and economic change. In Kenya, much of the independence struggle was about land; the official name of the "Mau Mau" rebellion movement was the Land Freedom Army. In the wake of independence in 1963, thousands of landless Kenyans gained access to land. Administration of the shift of land from European to African farmers was accomplished with remarkable alacrity. But even so, there were slippages. Well-positioned elite gained access to disproportionate quantities of land, often through devious means.

Discussion and action on the land issue was fostered by strong indigenous emotions. The journey of the land issue from an "emotion" through a political process to a "commodity" continued long after the immediate independence period. In various ways, the churches through the NCCK contributed creatively to the "land" issue by drawing on biblical models as well as aspects of customary land tenure and ownership models.

Food

In 1980, Kenya spent more than 470 million shillings to purchase food in foreign markets. According to a 1981 sessional paper, the food deficit was predicted to continue until the end of the decade. Thus, the foreign exchange to be spent on food during the following nine years would be phenomenal and potentially crippling.

The reasons for this food-deficit build-up were related to factors such as population pressure, an agricultural system requiring foreign inputs, a decline in the nurture of indigenous foods, and the complicated sojourn of land tenure in Kenya. In some sense, the food deficit could be understood as a byproduct of the modern development process. It was further assumed that, inasmuch as food required monitoring, it could be done on a political basis. These have proven to be faulty assumptions. With their widespread rural network, it was hard to imagine that churches could avoid involvement with food issues in the foreseeable future.

Tradition as Resource

Given the experience to date, it would seem that the single largest blind spot in the so-called development process centered on indigenous knowledge. At best, these resources were ignored. At worst, indigenous wisdom was viewed as a constraint to development.

The modern development process made an assumption that the non-Western world would trade in its wisdom accumulated over millennia for technical tools and systems of relatively recent origin. The trade-off resulted in mixed benefits, requiring serious continued monitoring and evaluation.

Meanwhile, indigenous knowledge needed to be revisited, distilling what was appropriate for the future. Several areas suggested themselves for urgent attention:

1. *Nutrition.* The collective memory of rural Kenya was neglected, and was being lost in significant measure. Some of this loss became apparent in the form of food deficits.
2. *Trees.* In Kenya, the modern forestry system was informed largely by exotic (foreign) trees. The whole system only furtively touched on indigenous knowledge regarding trees. The gap between the two could to some extent be measured in the prevailing rural energy deficit and the ongoing deforestation.
3. *Indigenous knowledge with regard to pastoralism.* Modern ranching systems in Maasailand drew heavily on indigenous pastoral wisdom. In the late 1970s, pastoral systems in northern Kenya had been

influenced only marginally by modern husbandry and marketing systems. There was, for example, much scope and promise in the recognition, breeding, and selection of camels. A market for camel milk seemed promising.

VIII. Postures for the Future

Toward a Catalytic Role

In the life of the churches and in the life of the nation, the NCCK played many roles. One could mention the advocacy role, the service role, the coordinating role, and the liaison role with the Kenyan government and with all manner of overseas organizations.

Such roles and relationships were nurtured and sustained for many reasons, typically assuming the form of a project or a well-focused activity. Given the growing capacity of the NCCK member churches on the one hand, and the debilitating weight of project and institutional maintenance on the other, a case could be made in favor of the administratively lighter role of catalyst.

Borrowing from the world of chemistry, the catalyst role is that of enabling the separate parts of a chemical mixture to interact. A similar role could be played by the NCCK in the life of the church community. Properly done, such a role would have the potential of enlarging and mobilizing the talents of the church community. More specifically, such a role would suggest a much closer interaction between the NCCK as an organizational institution and the life of the churches.

Toward Criteria for Receiving Overseas Aid

Over the years, projects within the NCCK were funded by a plethora of overseas donors. Each of the donors established and followed specific, carefully contrived criteria for aid giving and receiving. The NCCK as recipient was expected to meet those often-disparate criteria.

Based on the experience in the Rural Development Department, it became clear that it was simply impossible to meet the many different donor demands for audited financial statements, evaluations, and quantifications of project performance. Taken collectively, those criteria canceled each other out. They became meaningless as valid guides toward helpful development or change activity. The challenge for the churches was to develop their own criteria for receiving aid and for determining whether and how the selected projects had achieved desirable goals.

Toward a Change Dialogue

Inasmuch as there was any ongoing reflection process, it took place in the districts. The various NCCK coordinating committees mentioned in the report did their work, sometimes very well. They facilitated discussion with the "village," with member churches, and with government offices.

If these forums represented and exercised any genius, it can be attributed to their diversity. By contrast, the discussion at the national level were definitely found wanting. The 3Rs Committee agendas were preoccupied with the Rural Training Center agendas. Attempts to bring church representatives into a discussion of national rural issues were generally unsuccessful. By the same token, relationships with government departments on the national level were less than satisfactory.

The postindependence years from 1974 to 1981, the period of my tenure with the NCCK's Rural Development Department, were characterized by a sense of urgency: everything was priority. While all things seemed possible, not all goals were achievable. Skill levels and readily applicable research findings were growing exponentially, but not adequately available to the skill levels, opportunities, and urgencies at hand. At a personal level, those years and the issues engaged with were stimulating beyond measure. Future historians must judge the validity and utility of the goals, energies, and resources that were formulated and expended.

—*May 1981*

8
Darfur Ecumenical Visit

March 25 to April 3, 2008

Introduction

The World Council of Churches sponsored a pastoral visit by an ecumenical delegation comprising church representatives ("living letters") from diverse parts of the world to demonstrate solidarity with the churches of Sudan. During this ten-day visit, members of the delegation were formed into small groups, which dispersed to preselected communities within Sudan. This report reflects the impressions of a four-member subgroup of the delegation that traveled to the town of Nyala in southern Darfur, a region in western Sudan.

Darfur was among the destinations chosen by the WCC for a small group visit because, among other reasons, of its persistent depiction in the media as one of the world's largest humanitarian crises. Described as an area equal to the size of France, Darfur was "home" to 2.5 million internally displaced people (IDPs) who lived in organized camps, variously serviced by international and Sudanese humanitarian agencies. According to some estimates, more than four million Darfurians had been adversely affected by armed conflict since 2003.

Grievances giving rise to armed conflict in Darfur can be traced to the 1890s. Since the 1600s, Darfur had existed as an independent sultanate, but was forcibly integrated by the Anglo-Egyptian Condominium government (1899–1956) of the day with the Sudan territory. When independence came to Sudan in 1956, Darfur's status as an integral part of the country remained unchanged.

In the meantime, popular discontent, especially among the agricultural communities in Darfur, had been simmering. By 2003, rebel groups—initially the Sudan Liberation Movement (SLM) and the Joint Equity Movement (JEM)—engaged in armed resistance to perceived oppressive central government policies. Subsequently, the Reform and Development Movement (RDM) became one of numerous splinter rebel groups. In response to this uprising, the government of Sudan mobilized Arab militias, the so-called *janjaweed*—armed horsemen from among semi-nomadic pastoralist—to quell the rebellion. As of this writing, the political situation in Darfur has become complex beyond ready comprehension, with rebel groups—"mutineers"—switching and rearranging allegiances in opportunist fashion. Hence the difficulty of identifying reliable partners for any authentic negotiating exercise toward a viable peace agreement.

It was understood that Darfur's resistance movements were inspired initially by the protracted, but eventually successful, armed resistance of the Sudan People's Liberation Movement (SPLM) in South Sudan, led by the late John Garang de Mabior. They were inspired as well by the provisions of the negotiated resolution of the conflict in South Sudan, known as the Comprehensive Peace Agreement (CPA), signed in January 2005 between the Sudan Government and the SPLM. For some years, the African Union provided the framework within which protracted negotiations toward the resolution of grievances variously expressed by Darfur's dissident movements had been conducted. Supplementary efforts in this regard were undertaken by the then current SPLM government of South Sudan. As of this writing, these undertakings toward a peaceful settlement of Darfur's conflicts were ongoing.

Hosted in Nyala Town

The four-member WCC team arrived in Nyala on March 27, where it was graciously hosted by staff of the Darfur Emergency Response Operation (DERO), an ecumenical consortium formed as a result of initiatives by ACT International and Caritas Internationalis. Norwegian Church Aid (NCA), as a member organization of ACT, served as the officially registered entity in Sudan on behalf of DERO. The Sudan Council of Churches (SCC) with both Protestant and Catholic membership; SudanAid, a humanitarian agency of the Catholic Church in Sudan; and the Sudan

Social Development Organization (SUDO), a secular human rights cum humanitarian agency, were deemed to function as DERO's local Sudanese collaborating partner agencies.

The ACT-Caritas presence in Darfur was supported by more than sixty donors, including agencies and governments. ACT comprised a global alliance of Protestant and Orthodox aid agencies, while Caritas comprised agencies from the Roman Catholic community. Together, the ACT Alliance and the Caritas network represented the majority of the Christian faith-based humanitarian aid agencies, with a presence in many countries around the world. In Darfur, DERO had focused on emergency humanitarian response, with the understanding that certain humanitarian services offered in the IDP camps would be provided by DERO's local Sudanese partner agencies. The WCC delegation to Darfur took note that SCC, SudanAid, and Sudo had been operational in Darfur prior to the formation of DERO. At the time of the visit, SCC's field program was in abeyance and undergoing review. Because of security concerns in Darfur and because of SCC's restructuring exercise, the DERO emergency humanitarian program had not kept pace with the originally proposed implementation schedule. It was considered that the DERO consortium constituted an experiment of a particular model of ecumenical cooperation.

Because of increasingly insecure conditions in Darfur, especially in the southern and western regions, DERO's international staff were grounded at the time of the visit, confined for all practical purposes to the NCA compound in Nyala town. Insecurity was characterized by hijacking of vehicles—some of which was understood as bandit activity—belonging to humanitarian agencies, including two DERO vehicles. Further complicating matters were the Sudan government's security restrictions, applicable in particular to DERO's international staff. Such staff members were not being issued with work visas, or with exit visas to facilitate leave or vacation time away from field duty in Darfur. Thus, at the time of the delegation visit, DEROs international staff were not in a position to stay, to work, or to leave!

DERO's acting director, together with his colleagues, provided an overview of the situation with which they were engaged in Darfur. Protracted armed conflict had seriously and negatively affected the financial contributions from ecumenical and government donors, as well as the general morale of the DERO staff. Local authorities imposed onerous administrative obstacles on the work of NGOs active in the region, seriously impeding effective delivery of humanitarian services. In the months prior to our visit, the largest number of armed clashes had been limited to western Darfur; however, random banditry had become an endemic problem in southern Darfur.

Since October 2007, seventy-one WFP trucks and two NCA vehicles had been hijacked, with thirty WFP drivers unaccounted for. Meanwhile, armed attacks on NGO compounds had become commonplace. Security in the IDP camps had deteriorated alarmingly, with rapes and violent clashes taking place on virtually a daily basis. At the same time, reports indicated that nomads from Chad, Niger, and elsewhere were being invited to settle in Darfur, in villages and on farms previously occupied by civilians who now lived in camps for internally displaced people. Any eventual repatriation of IDPs to their original homes was therefore in serious jeopardy.

Due to security considerations, the WCC team was obliged to remain in the DERO compound during the two-day visit in Nyala. The visit was thus limited to meetings with the DERO management team, with their national partners (SCC, SudanAid, and SUDO), and with the church leaders of the region. On the final day of the visit, just before departure, it became possible to visit a women's center in Nyala town, funded by the Danish Embassy. The center offered space for women of the town to meet and exchange views on matters of special concern to women. It also functioned as an adult education center for women, touching on a wide range of issues common to situations in urban Sudan.

Meanwhile, the deployment of UNAMID in Darfur did not seem to have appreciably improved the situation on the ground. Their limitations in terms of logistics did not allow them to have a serious impact on the prevailing insecurities, which only added to the general mistrust on the part of the local population.

Meeting with DERO's National Partners

In a meeting with DERO's national partners—SCC, SudanAid, and SUDO—the team was informed about the humanitarian assistance being undertaken. Most of the services offered by the local partners fell within the DERO mandate. However, the local partners also undertook activities considered to be outside the DERO mandate, in part because the local Sudanese agencies had been operational in the region prior to the establishment of DERO. According to a strategic plan, DERO was intended to have ceded its program to the national partners by mid-2008. However, this plan was acknowledged as unrealistic. A strategic review called for strengthening the capacity of the national partner agencies. The latter expressed their desire for the DERO program to be eventually handed over to them, and also expressed their appreciation for the appointment, upon their request, of an international accompanier to enhance their implementing capacity.

Meeting with Church Leaders

The team had opportunity to meet with members of the Inter-Church Committee (ICC), comprising leaders of Christian faith communities active in Darfur: the Evangelical, Catholic, Pentecostal, Episcopal, and Coptic churches. After the signing of the CPA, churches in Nyala town had been enjoying a considerable measure of religious freedom. They had not been subjected to any discriminatory measures. Churches had access to their own plots of land; however, due to financial limitations they were unable to build on all of the available plots. Therefore, the churches were renting houses that functioned as worship facilities.

In 2006, SudanAid invited leaders from both Christian and Muslim communities to participate in a workshop. Following this encounter, a peacebuilding committee to promote interfaith dialogue was created, and convened a number of meetings. Unfortunately, it had been difficult to convene regular meetings due to financial constraints. Churches were actively involved in humanitarian work, providing assistance to people in various IDP camps. Church leaders also stressed the need to support and promote educational programs for the benefit of women and youth in the region. Finally, they expressed the wish to strengthen relationships with the SCC, which was in the process of restructuring its presence in the region after an absence occasioned by programmatic and administrative difficulties.

Meeting the Director of the Nyala Town Center for Women

The center for women had been established with financing from the Danish Embassy. It was active in the fields of peacebuilding, protection, development, psychological support, and empowerment for women by means of training and encounter. According to the director, the center was operated exclusively by women for women. With its open-door policy, the center had managed to gain the trust of the local population, providing women with an acceptable meeting place where training for employment opportunities was on offer. It was the plan of the management to bring the whole of the center's program under the direction of members of the local community.

Observations

Darfur was at once the site of one of the world's largest humanitarian crises and the site of protracted and complex armed conflict. Both the humanitarian crisis and that portion of the crisis manifest as armed conflict straddled the border with neighboring Chad. Both crises were fueled and rendered complex by growing ecological deterioration, thus enhancing the competition, respectively, for suitable farming and grazing land. It was generally considered that these complex crises could not be resolved militarily, even though it was clear that they had been influenced by military action from various quarters, including the governments of Chad and Sudan in the form of armed militia and armed rebels. All aspects of these multiple crises were infused with political implications and needed to be addressed by carefully designed and well-balanced peace negotiations.

Since November 2006, the United Nations and the African Union (AU), led respectively by mediators Jan Eliasson and Salim Salim, had been mandated to reinvigorate the formal peace process. Although they claimed success in bringing the rebels together and reducing the number of rebel factions from approximately twenty to five, the most influential rebel leaders (Abdul Wahid of SLA and Kahlil Ibrahim of JEM) refused to come to the negotiating table. Attempts to hold talks in Sirte, Libya, were abandoned only two days after launch due to a boycott of the meeting by rebel leaders critical to the process.

For the global ecumenical community, the Darfur calamity presented a huge challenge. The DERO undertaking, described briefly above, represented an attempt by the ecumenical community to respond to a colossal humanitarian crisis. At the time of the WCC visitation, this globally constituted consortium, drawing support from faith-based organizations and governments in sixty countries, was for all practical purposes grounded because of security considerations.

On the other hand, the WCC team was repeatedly reminded throughout the visit to Sudan of the CPA-related peace process. During a debriefing with representatives of the AU in Khartoum (including Abdul Mohammed), the team was told that the CPA is the "policy framework which holds the Sudan together." In a briefing session with representatives of SUDO in Nyala, the WCC team was told that the CPA provided the framework within which Sudanese civil society groups, including SUDO, were steadily increasing the scope and space for their humanitarian and human rights activities.

In his keynote address presented to the two-day seminar in Juba, the Rev. Dr. Sam Kobia, General Secretary of the World Council of Churches, recounted in careful detail the nature of the accompaniment by the ecumenical community—both global and Sudanese—with the development and eventual signing of the CPA. Rev. Kobia's comments were corroborated with much appreciation by a senior official of the SPLM government of South Sudan in his public presentation to the ecumenical seminar.

It became obvious to the Darfur team that the contribution of the ecumenical community to the formation and still-incomplete implementation of the CPA represented a notable landmark in the region's slow but steady transformation over the past decades. It was also acknowledged by both Sudanese church and government representatives that the actual implementation of the CPA ("that which holds Sudan together") had been dogged by complications and disappointments.

Advocacy choices for the ecumenical community with regard to Sudan were rather stark. There was a need to consider a greatly strengthened ecumenical accompaniment with and support for a full implementation of the CPA. Despite its faults, the CPA held considerable promise for Sudan generally, and for Darfur and South Sudan particularly, as well as for other marginalized areas of this vast land.

Ecumenical veterans recalled precedent from the Biafran War in the 1960s. The huge ecumenical humanitarian consortium in Biafra had been confronted sooner than expected with a peace option—thanks to the work of a lone Quaker peacemaker. Faced with a sudden demise in the demand for humanitarian services, the sponsors of the ecumenical consortium proposed to the then General Secretary of the All Africa Conference of Churches: "Could the Biafra ecumenical humanitarian apparatus be transferred to South Sudan to cater for the emerging humanitarian needs developing around the Anya Nya rebel campaign?" (What a pity to close down a well-oiled humanitarian apparatus!) Canon Burgess Carr, the AACC General Secretary, replied, "I would rather try the peace option!"

While history never repeats itself precisely, the similarities between Biafra and Sudan are nevertheless intriguing. Even in its present form and in the present state of implementation, the CPA invited greatly enhanced ecumenical engagement and support. At the very least, the ecumenical-humanitarian combine in Darfur would have done well to diversify and devolve its portfolio, adopting smaller, more agile institutional formats, which could provide support to peace efforts, on the one hand, and be open to collaboration with humanitarian agencies from the Arab/Muslim world on the other.

Throughout the WCC's solidarity visit to Sudan, the international media reported on ongoing campaigns, especially in North Atlantic countries, to "Save Darfur." Debate regarding the most appropriate ways and means of demonstrating concern for the resolution of the Darfur conundrum and for the full and equitable implementation of the CPA persisted. Given the remarkable track record of ecumenical accompaniment with Sudan's peace process, there seemed to be a self-evident case for strengthening the ability of the ecumenical church community (nationally, regionally, and internationally) to continue its support for a peaceful and just Sudan.

—Christina Papazoglou and Harold F. Miller
April 16, 2008

WCC Delegates on Darfur Visit

- Christina Papazoglou, WCC staff person, Geneva
- Fred Nyabara, director of FECCLAHA, Nairobi
- Fred Nzwili, journalist, Nairobi
- Harold F. Miller, seconded by Mennonite Central Committee to the All Africa Conference of Churches 1989–1999

Note: This field visit report was drafted by Christina Papazoglou, augmented and finalized by Harold F. Miller, commented on by Fred Nzwili, and approved by Fred Nyabara. Permission to reprint this piece was given by Marianne Ejdersten, WCC Director for Communications.

9
Development as Exotica

THE YOUNG PASTOR was leading the conversation through a maze of traditional names. People of his ethnic group, he explained, take on different names as they pass through the age-group rituals. He was obviously well versed in local tradition and seemed to take great pride in his ethnocultural roots. Later that day, he showed us around his village, and among other things pointed out a tree that in the past had saved his people from the ravages of drought. The plum-sized fruit of the tree was eaten; the branches were used as livestock fodder. Even in normal times, the tree had its uses, he noted. Gum that oozed from the cracks in the trunk was used as an adhesive to attach arrowheads to shafts. Some forms of the gum possessed medicinal value. In short, the tree had been integral to the survival traditions of the people who lived along the western wall of the Great Rift Valley.

In the midst of this rather rustic traditional setting, we spotted examples of recognizable modern-sector development. We toured the riverside factory processing fluorspar, being mined from a huge gash in the distant valley wall. Fluorspar is a mineral used in the production of steel. Downstream from the factory there was overwhelming evidence of river pollution. In the village, we found modern houses for workers and a health clinic that served factory workers, as well as members of the community at large.

A short distance from the mineral extraction site was an irrigated fruit and vegetable farm, featuring exotic trees of many varieties from Australia and Latin America. But the tree that had served the people of this valley in times of drought was nowhere to be seen. Indeed, when the farm supervisor, a trained agriculturist and forester, was asked why the local tree was not included among the trees of the farm, it became clear that he saw no relationship between "development" and the promotion of that traditionally valuable tree.

*

According to the United Nations calendar, the Second Development Decade (the 1970s) was coming to a close. "Development" was the term used to describe the process by which so-called third world nations were to be eased into the mainstream of the modern world. The early 1960s had marked the demise of European colonialism in Africa. In its wake rose politically independent nation-states. Those transition years had also given birth to the concept of development as a recognizable, modernizing process. Much of the subsequent momentum in that regard had been provided by the United Nations and its specialized agencies. But if the United Nations agencies had served as midwives of the development dynamic, a host of voluntary, nongovernmental agencies, including Christian mission and service agencies, had become frontline exponents of the process as well. Indeed, Christian missions had provided much more than mere development footmen. During the great missionary century—from the mid-1800s to the mid-1900s—Christian missions had laid the foundation for significant portions of what is today acknowledged as development activity. Many missionary kids (children of missionaries) found their way into some specialized United Nations development agency or with a nongovernmental organization (NGO), enjoying a running start as an experienced "Third Worlder."

In evaluating the achievements of the First Development Decade (the 1960s), Dr. Robert Gardinier, a distinguished African serving as a United Nations official, noted that the most important, if not the only, positive breakthrough in Africa's rural development had been accomplished by Christian missionaries and related service agencies. Subsequently, Christian agencies of many hues had undertaken leading development roles in the third world.

Meanwhile the development process had come under increasing scrutiny. What, finally, was the fruit of Western-style development on the African continent? At what cost was such development being appropriated? Did the "benefits" of development reach the least privileged, the poorest of the world? What happened to people in Africa who experienced some version of the development process? One conspicuous result of the process could be observed in that corps of educated elite throughout third world countries, who increasingly spoke the same academic, cultural, and consumer languages. They had become citizens of the modern world, as much at home in London as in Nairobi. Such people raised their children to speak only English (or French or Portuguese). These were children who could not communicate with their grandmothers in mother tongue languages, who hesitated to visit Grandmother in the village because her compound featured no flush toilet. Among them were malnourished children with access to all manner of sweets, with teeth sporting cavities even before the age of ten.

Missiologists avow that third world Christians, in rejecting their former belief systems and traditions, run the risk of rejecting themselves. For example, until today many African Christians have difficulty accepting drums in a church service because of the earlier association of drums with certain indigenous African religious and cultural beliefs. Such rejection of the use of drums constituted, in some sense, a rejection of the core of African music—rhythm. In some African communities, drumming had for a long time been associated with healing. It was a rejection that kept all things aesthetic and religious slightly off balance. How could solid foundations for the future be constructed when self-rejection was at work and self-identity uncertain?

Some missiologists accepted such anomalous tensions as integral, even necessary, to the normal transition from an old to a new socio-religious order. Others raised questions. Does any people really have the capacity to shift from one cultural or spiritual order to another without major societal disruptions and breakdowns? Perhaps such breakdowns were deemed to be among the normal costs of church planting. On the other hand, could it be assumed that all peoples were aware of the creator God long before the missionaries appeared on the scene? Could Christian belief patterns be built upon select insights of the traditional religious heritage? For some missiologists and for certain African theologians, the answers to these two questions were decidedly "yes." According to them, there existed complementary relationships between indigenous African religious belief systems and the Christian understanding of God, begging for recognition and affirmation.

Meanwhile, the building of bridges between the old and the new became an active concern in Africa. When a people forfeits its own history, are they by intent or default questioning God's presence and purpose in that history? Are they questioning their validity as a people? It has generally been assumed by a segment of the Christian missionary fraternity that the Christian gospel constitutes good news to every culture, to the peculiar religio-cultural idiom of every people. Others viewed the missionary witness simply as transplanted alien agenda.

As in Christian evangelism, some of the so-called development patterns have been unwieldy, if for purposes of this reflection arbitrary distinctions can be drawn between diverse operational modes. In its crudest form, development has been a Western economic agenda imposed on all kinds of non-Western situations. The development process began with the insights and the expertise of the "change agent": the missionary, the service worker, the expert. For example, development introduced the exotic "grade" cow—a euphemism for the purebred or semi-purebred cows from Europe or America—together with all the supporting apparatus in the form of stringent management systems. Another example: dominant among the trees that characterized the white settler farms in Kenya was the exotic eucalyptus tree from Australia. Thus did the eucalyptus tree become an accepted development symbol, while the indigenous counterparts were ignored and neglected. The introduction of development exotica helped to ease a new economy into the rural areas of Africa. Cash crops such as coffee were successfully introduced. Earnings from such crops provided access to a vast array of Western capital and consumer goods. But with time, cash crops competed with food crops and wood-fuel lots. While the coffee boom attracted significant foreign exchange for certain African countries, it inclined some people to make do with less fuel wood—95 percent of rural energy in Kenya is accessed in the form of wood—and with less variety in the food diet.

Many of Kenya's communities formerly included all manner of leafy greens in their traditional diets. In some areas, such greens have been replaced by cabbage—an import to Africa and a decidedly inferior substitute, according to nutritionists. Some indigenous forests were replaced by fast-growing exotic (foreign-sourced) trees. The transition occasioned loss of exclusive flora and fauna, to say nothing of the loss of the ecological and other "services" provided by indigenous forests. Development, like the Christianizing process, has been characterized by selective rejection of the indigenous in favor of the exotic.

Happily, a shift in the development mode can be discerned. It is being sensed and acknowledged that valid development must be built upon the resources and the understanding of the affected community. Authentic development calls for identifying and beginning with resources immediately available, strengthening the positive with accompanying development research focused on local trees, on indigenous livestock, on local knowledge of all kinds. Every local situation must be acknowledged as valid. Indeed, any genuine development processes must be premised on the creative deployment of local resources.

This shift in the development enterprise might be called the "barefootization" of development. It is an insight borrowed from China, emphasizing the creative deployment of existing local knowledge and skills. This concept has already inspired a global change in the approach to health care—a shift from the curative to community-based, primary health care. Similarly, a new worldwide afforestation network is basing its research initially on local knowledge of local trees. According to some development wisdom, it may be better to select "upward" from indigenous livestock and to interbreed only selectively with exotic cattle rather than to replace local indigenous stock entirely. The current development tilt constitutes an attempt to keep local people and local resources at the center of the development process. It is, in short, an effort to move development away from exotica and toward that which a so-called developing community could identify as "us" or "ours."

If development is understood only as an attempt to "meet human need," it may be time for a rethink. "Need" is to a large extent culturally determined. Americans know that certain needs become apparent if they are sufficiently stimulated by advertisements. Some needs are intrinsic to human survival. The difference between the several kinds of needs has become confused in the development process. Perhaps that was inevitable.

Christians in "developing" countries, as well as those in "developed" countries, are becoming aware of a common agenda. For example, the land controversy is everywhere at the center of the development discussion. How to buy, sell, zone, cultivate, and inherit land are problems common to Kenyan Mennonites and to American Mennonites. Admittedly, there are cultural variations, but the basic issues are similar.

Food is another example. In Third World countries, there is a tendency toward mono-diets, partly in response to the competing cash crops. Americans are consuming fast, convenient foods. In both cases, the result is some degree of malnourishment.

In many ways, development has come home to roost. It is remarkable that American Mennonites have only within the relatively recent past begun a serious conversation regarding the stewardship of land. The phenomenal success of the *More-with-Less* cookbook suggested a fresh concern with good food. As with most Mennonite issues, the discussion soon assumed a theological turn. What is the biblical basis for our land and food concerns—that is, for our development concerns? Hope for our own creative involvement in the development process, anywhere, lies in this new inquiry. For us, development is no longer exotica. It has become a living issue in the life of the worldwide Christian community.

Published in the August 1979 edition of *Missionary Messenger* (Eastern Mennonite Board of Missions).

10
Ecumenical Dimensions in Africa

Introduction

March 31, 1999, marked the conclusion of my ten-year secondment by the Mennonite Central Committee (MCC) to the staff of the International Affairs Desk of the All Africa Conference of Churches (AACC), having served for the duration as a "consultant" (mostly "jack-of-a-variety-of-trades"). Those years with AACC must be added to a seven-year term (1974-81) with the National Council of Churches of Kenya (NCCK), a one-and-a-half-year period (1973-74) with Sudan Council of Churches (SCC), and six years (1965-71) with the Christian Council of Tanzania (CCT), the latter three assignments on secondment from Eastern Mennonite Board of Missions (EMM). Together, these years can be understood as a gesture of fraternal solidarity by two North American Mennonite agencies with the African Protestant ecumenical community.

Mennonite origins are traced to the free church tradition, whereas the mainline Protestant missionary-founded churches in Africa trace their origins, in significant measure, to European state-church traditions. Against that backdrop, how were the secondments to "mainline" ecumenical bodies rationalized? And how were MCC's long-term relationships with a number of African Christian Councils understood? To my knowledge, those questions were not seriously entertained within the Mennonite mission and service fraternity.

From a personal perspective, the reasons for the open collaboration between MCC and African ecumenical entities could be located in the nature of the role of "church" in Africa during that unprecedented political and ecclesial transition period in the early 1960s, when the dynamics of *"uhuru"* (political independence and its ecclesial counterpart) were everywhere astir. Subsequently, the continent encountered important issues that "church" was uniquely placed to address: "By seeing Christ at work in the emerging African states, [the African ecumenical church] tied that cosmic figure to African political and economic aspirations, a link that has remained unbroken to this day" (Utuk 1997).

"Church" as an ecumenical expression in sub-Saharan Africa served as a kind of halfway house between the continent's indigenous religious heritage and the emerging sociopolitical order. With their strong sacral proclivities, Africans readily endorsed that which referred to the creator God in the missionary message, on the one hand, and readily accessed, on the other, the doors opened by the "missionary-founded church" into Western-style education and thus into critical engagement with formal-sector economic and governance systems bequeathed or variously imposed by the colonial order.

My engagement with Africa's ecumenical community over a three-decade period was that of a sojourner and student, accompanying a project that was finding its way into a postcolonial future. At a personal level, it was an enormously enriching experience and it was, for all practical purposes, a front-row seat on an African drama. The remainder of this reflection touches on issues that served, from my limited perspective, to focus the ecumenical agenda and to inform the key roles played by the ecumenical community during this particularly dynamic period of Africa's modern emergence.

East African Setting

My perspective onto Africa's ecumenical community was lodged primarily in East Africa, though the AACC mandate offered a continental overview. At the time (1965) of our arrival in Tanzania, Mennonite missionaries had just experienced several decades of intense engagement with the East African Revival Movement, a spiritual renewal phenomenon that facilitated "Christian fellowship" across a broad confessional and societal spectrum. Indeed, the distinctions between "ecumenical" and "evangelical" faith traditions had been rendered permeable throughout this period thanks to the interdenominational character of the Revival Movement. "Church-and-society" issues during this transition time were widely recognized as important and urgent by an equally broad spectrum of churches in East Africa. Typically, archbishops in the Anglican church (widely acknowledged, nominally and informally, as the "state church" in East Africa), as well as heads of other mainline Protestant churches, were ardent adherents of the East Africa Revival Fellowship and also deeply engaged with the political, liberation, and development issues of the day.

For purposes at hand, the Rev. Dr. John Gatu, for many years the moderator ("Archbishop") of the Presbyterian Church in East Africa, served as the model churchperson of the day. He was an active member of the East Africa Revival Fellowship; he was also instrumental in the indigenization of the NCCK, thus facilitating the shift from missionary to African leadership, and an active participant in the group of Kenyan church leaders who initiated pre-independence contact—despite hesitation among missionaries of the day—with the much-maligned nationalist leader, Jomo Kenyatta, then being held in detention by the colonial government in northern Kenya.

Like other self-confident East African Christians, Gatu refused to live according to strictures imposed by the Western missionary fraternity. Together with other church leaders, he embodied a remarkable ability to embrace and bridge the respective ecumenical/evangelical, nationalist/ecclesial, evangelistic/social action, high/low church dichotomies. In the early 1970s, he emerged as a strong advocate for a moratorium on the missionary presence in Africa and the attendant influence and monetary support from "mother churches" in Europe and North America. Gatu was instrumental during the famous Lausanne, Switzerland, Conference of Evangelicals (1974) in deflecting plans for the establishment of a global evangelical church body, intended at the time as a counter organization to the World Council of Churches. From Gatu's perspective, the evangelical community in the Western world had not been present to the African continent in its most critical hour. In notable contrast to the global ecumenical community, it had not been supportive of Africa's struggle for political and ecclesial independence at a time when those issues had served as preconditions to any forward movement for the religious, social, and political development of the African continent.

For many years, he was engaged ecumenically and continentally with the AACC at the level of its executive committee. He was also a strong Kenyan patriot, having endorsed the nationalist movement toward freedom, while at the same time taking strong exception to what he considered inappropriate nationalist oathing ceremonies conducted within his own Kikuyu community. In that cauldron of diverse and competing loyalties, he wrote a gracious foreword to a book *(Ambushed by Love: God's Triumph in Kenya's Terror)* authored by Mennonite missionary Dorothy Smoker, in which she reported on research regarding the suffering of "nonresistant" Revival Fellowship Christians amid what were deemed by some church leaders of the day to be the excesses of Kenya's rebel anticolonial, pro-independence Mau Mau movement.

Such were the personalities and atmospherics within which the Christian Councils of Kenya and Tanzania, and, more broadly, the continental context in which the AACC functioned at the time. For the administrators of both EMM and MCC, the African ecumenical entities provided convenient points of engagement with an emerging indigenized church community in East Africa and beyond, even though the term "ecumenical" was viewed askance, at the time, within their respective North American Mennonite constituencies.

Ecumenical Initiative

Political Independence

The release on February 11, 1990, of Nelson Mandela after twenty-seven years of incarceration under South Africa's apartheid government, fitted into place a key piece of the continent's independence dynamic, a process in sub-Saharan Africa that had begun with Ghana in 1957. Mandela's installation on April 27, 1994, as the first president of South Africa emerging from the country's African majority marked the end of over three hundred years of European minority rule, the final forty-six of which had been guided by the separatist or racist policies of the National Party, dominated by Afrikaners of Dutch descent. South Africa was thus joining the community of politically independent nations in Africa and in the world, affixing the structures of democratic governance that ostensibly included everyone to what was being referred to as the "rainbow nation." In consequence, an electric, magical moment in the history of Africa, and indeed in the world beyond, was celebrated.

At a critical juncture in the anti-apartheid movement, a relatively obscure Anglican clergyman by the name of Desmond Tutu had been tapped on the shoulder by senior ecumenical personalities—including several African church leaders—of the World Council of Churches. He was being urged to provide focus for the growing anti-apartheid movement. As recalled by the Rev. Jose Chipenda, General Secretary of the AACC, in personal communication with me, Tutu at first demurred: "You people from outside South Africa do not understand our complex situation." But the representatives of the ecumenical community would not accept no for an answer. They commissioned Tutu to work proactively for a post-apartheid, majority-rule government in South Africa. And the rest, as the adage goes, is history. In profound ways, Tutu served as a bridge between the political and theological quest for South Africa's liberation. Eventually he became Africa's best-known church-related personality, honored with the Nobel Peace Prize, which he accepted on behalf of Africans across the continent and in the African diaspora.

Tutu's tenure brought to fruition a number of African dreams. There had been the Pan-Africanist dream of a politically independent continent, articulated already in the late 1800s by academics and activists among the Afro-Caribbean diaspora. Beginning in 1900, those advocates had staged five major Pan-African Congresses that brought together young nationalist leaders from across the African continent into a common quest for political independence from European colonial rule. Among them were Kenyatta of Kenya and Nkrumah of Ghana. Also fulfilled in some measure were the dreams of the Organization of Africa Unity (established in 1963, comprised of heads of independent African nation states) and its Liberation Committee, chaired by President Julius Nyerere of Tanzania, who also served at the time as chair of the Organization of Front Line States, a united front of independent African states in support of the liberation movements in southern African countries still under the strictures of colonial or minority "white" (European settler) rule.

As the political liberation of the continent was realized, so also, in significant measure, was the vision of the ecumenical community fulfilled. In the 1974 General Assembly, the general secretary of the AACC openly endorsed the armed resistance deemed necessary for the liberation of southern Africa. Some African Christian leaders expressed umbrage vis-à-vis the general secretary's specific endorsement of violence, as did some overseas partners of the AACC. Early leaders of the AACC had at times remonstrated against what was considered an excessive preoccupation among leaders of member churches with "nationalism." "Liberation," on the other hand, was understood in African ecumenical circles as a theological concept, embracing aspirations of the state, the church, and the continent's religious and cultural heritage.

While the fundamental urge for liberation was rarely in question, the related theological reflection as pursued in the ecumenical community was considered in some quarters of the church to be risky or even heretical. For some ecumenical partners who traced their beginnings to the radical sixteenth-century Reformation tradition that called for the separation of church and state, engagement with the African liberation project during this time was embraced in uneven, cautious fashion. For those partners, engagement with issues related to the relatively risk-free issues of diaconal and socioeconomic development was more readily embraced. Did the more restricted focus of certain ecumenical partners miss or underestimate the import of the critical content and implications of the larger liberation project, thus reflecting a major lacuna in the understanding of the African story during this momentous century? Possibly. This end-of-century juncture provided occasion to revisit some of the more contentious issues.

Independence Aftermath

The African church in its ecumenical form and in its modern, recognizably Western institutional garb, played an important role in the independence movement on the African continent. In that posture, the protagonists included Africans with strong Western-style education, on the one hand, pitted against the various colonial regimes on the other. In a straightforward contest, with Africans appealing for the most part to recognizable Western values of democracy, human rights, and basic Christian decency, it was only a matter of time till the African case against Western colonialism would be vindicated. Indeed, the outcome was never in doubt. But in the postindependence period—realized more fully after April 1994—Africa was faced with a virtually new continental situation.

The end of apartheid and the end of the independence struggle did not mark the beginning of a new tranquility in Africa. In fact, those punctuation points merely marked the end of "round one" in the quest for a reconstituted continent. The attainment of majority rule in South Africa in April 1994, it was noted repeatedly, coincided with the onset of genocide in Rwanda. Rwanda's genocidal explosion, in which an estimated eight hundred thousand people were killed in hand-to-hand combat, had portended a series of new conflicts and the intensification of existing ones. The larger global context was provided by the immediate post–Cold War period, the political ripples of which could be felt everywhere across the African continent.

Coining New Metaphors

At the end of March 1990, in light of the momentous changes that were taking place in his country and across Africa, Archbishop Desmond Tutu, the AACC's chair (1987–97), called for the coining of a biblical metaphor more appropriate to the times. Until then, the term "exile in Egypt" had served in common ecumenical parlance as the metaphor describing life under colonialism. The challenge was specifically assigned to Professor Jesse Mugambi, who subsequently developed and presented a paper to a meeting of the AACC's General Committee entitled "Beyond the Exodus and the Exile in Africa." In a book entitled *From Liberation to Reconstruction* (Nairobi. 1995. East African Educational Publishers), Mugambi set out the essential theological basis for the post-exilic metaphor of "reconstruction."

In a foreword to *Theology of Reconstruction: Exploratory Essays*, edited by Mary N. Getui and Emmanuel A. Obeng, Mugambi elaborated on the metaphor by citing the biblical character of Nehemiah, whose effort to rebuild the walls of Jerusalem served as the prototype of a "leader who represented the aspirations and contradictions of Africa's social reconstruction at this time in history." But if Nehemiah was the man and the rebuilt walls of Jerusalem the immediate prototypes for Africa's "reconstruction," upon which foundations was reconstruction to be commenced?

Mugambi dealt with such questions by revisiting the promises of the "secular city," as expounded by Harvey Cox in the 1960s ("Religion in Social Transformation" in *Democracy and Reconciliation: A Challenge for African Christianity*, edited by Laurenti Magesa and Zablon Nthamburi). During those modern optimistic days, there was an assumption that the indigenous sacral systems undergirding the African metaphysical and socioeconomic structures would slowly succumb to the emerging global "secular city." While African values had indeed been eroded by the modern globalization juggernaut, all had not been forgotten or lost. Of this, even Harvey Cox apparently became convinced after a visit to Africa. To paraphrase Kenya's John Mbiti, Africa continues to be a notoriously religious continent. As such, it was believed by many Africans to possess the moral and spiritual resources sufficient for rehabilitation, renewal, and "reconstruction."

Peace Initiatives

A partial list of Africa's postindependence unfinished business was readily assembled: the civil war in Liberia; the thrust of South Africa into Lesotho to quell a simmering military coup; the war in Sierra Leone; the armed attempt to oust President Mobutu in the Congo; the follow-up war to expel Rwanda and Uganda from the Congo; civil war in Burundi; the border war between Eritrea and Ethiopia; the perennial war between northern and southern Sudan, plus the auxiliary conflicts within northern and southern Sudan; the rebellion in northern Uganda; the continuing civil war in Angola; to say nothing of the collapsed state of Somalia, variously under the control of warlords and nascent substates.

Such was the bad news. And the bad news was rendered insidious by the not-so-subtle scramble by powerful multinational and African forces for the wealth of mineral-rich countries like the Congo. On the other hand, the fact that many of Africa's conflicts were being addressed or mediated by African-instituted peace initiatives was rarely acknowledged. In a number of those initiatives, members of the ecumenical community became involved in both catalytic and supportive roles. Collectively, those peace initiatives served as indicators of a reconstructing rather than a dying, despairing continent. And those initiatives were augmented by others, also of a positive nature.

Item: The Economic Community of West African States (ECOWAS) had mediated civil/regional wars in Liberia and Sierra Leone. In the case of Liberia, pivotal roles in the tortuous peace process had been played by an interfaith (Christian-Muslim) mediation committee. At its General Assembly in Addis Ababa, Ethiopia, in 1997, the AACC recognized this inter-faith collaboration for peace with the presentation of the Desmond Tutu Peace Prize to representatives of Liberia's Muslim and Christian communities, who had engaged in an interfaith initiative.

Item: The Inter-Governmental Agency for Development (IGAD) functioned as a seven-government forum for the Horn of Africa region focusing on development and conflict issues of common concern. Since 1993, it had also served as the official forum for the mediation of the civil war in Sudan. As an accompaniment to this formal forum, the AACC had convened periodic meetings from 1993 to 1997 of its Sudan Working Group, bringing together Nairobi-based agencies whose programs in various ways supported the quest for peace in Sudan.

Item: A "people-to-people peace initiative" by the New Sudan Council of Churches (NSCC) worked for peace between communities of South Sudan and thus strove to form an authentic basis for a more lasting peace within the whole of Sudan. This remarkable peace initiative undertaken by the NSCC enjoyed strong support from a broad range of politicians from South Sudan as well as wide recognition within the larger ecumenical community in Europe and North America.

Item: The Organization of African Unity had developed and launched a plan to resolve the Eritrean-Ethiopian border war. Representatives of the Fellowship of Churches and Christian Councils in the Great Lakes and Horn of Africa (FECCLAHA), the AACC, and the WCC made visits to the Orthodox and Lutheran (Mekane Yesu) churches in Ethiopia and Eritrea in an effort to move a reluctant peace process forward.

Item: The Southern Africa Development Community (SADC) exercised its mandate by intervening in conflicts within Lesotho and later in the Congo. Members of the Zambian government chaired negotiations focused on the complex Congo or Great Lakes War, and thus served as catalysts for the contentiously signed Lusaka Peace Accord. On the Congo-Rwanda-Uganda-Burundi war (sometimes referred to as the Great Lakes War or, more dramatically, as "Africa's First World War")—related in strange ways to conflicts in Sudan—individual churches and several Christian Councils, together with the AACC and the WCC, had intervened and made representations toward peaceful resolution.

Item: With a mandate from the Organization of African Unity (OAU), Julius Nyerere, president of Tanzania, had chaired the long-running negotiations in Arusha, Tanzania, between the government of Burundi and at least nineteen of the dissident Burundian political parties. OXFAM, the British NGO with Quaker origins, had served as the leading NGO support agency for those negotiations. Following Nyerere's death, the Burundi government had publicly declared its preference for South Africa as chair for the continuing negotiations.

Whence the energy, organization, and skilled personnel to undertake these arduous peacemaking tasks? Some portion of the vision for peace work could be credited to the much-cited and exhaustively analyzed South African Truth and Reconciliation Commission (TRC). Its formation at the behest of South Africa's president Nelson Mandela had sent a strong signal throughout the continent affirming that conflict could be resolved by means of peaceful negotiations. Additionally, Archbishop Tutu's high-profile position as the TRC's chairperson had given expression to the longstanding and continuing role of church in the resolution of historic grievances.

Due recognition had also to be given the broad mobilization of "civil society," both religious and secular, in the period following the demise of apartheid. This mobilization had been realized thanks to widespread training and "formation" in conflict resolution, a movement in which the churches and, especially, the National Christian Councils had been particularly active. In this regard, one of the earliest actors in peace work was the Nairobi Peace Initiative–Africa, founded in 1984 by individuals with experience and exposure as ecumenical activists. Subsequently, conflict-resolution work among churches and NGOs took on the dimensions of a "growth industry," a phenomenon mitigated later by the realities of attrition normally accompanying such bursts of enthusiasm.

Apart from these expressions of peace work, furtive references were made to the more latent impulses for a peaceful continent that seemed to be lodged somewhere within the metaphysic of African Religion, a source from which the African ecumenical movement had drawn much strength, albeit rather indirectly. That this was so can be verified by a careful reading of ecumenical treatises such as Utuk's *Visions of Authenticity* or Magesa's *African Religion: Moral Traditions for Abundant Life*.

But peace work, however widespread and however well done, could not be equated with "reconstruction." At best, peace work served only as a mediating, transitional process toward the realization of a reconstructed Africa. What were the reference points from which the reconstruction of the African continent could proceed? Again, Mugambi offered a broad-stroke analytic matrix. According to him, anyone concerned with the Africa of the future would need to reckon with the following major reference points that became clearly visible following the continental independence struggle.

- **African Religion (*Bantu Philosophy*):** Beginning in 1945 with the writings of Placid Tempels (*Bantu Philosophy*), serious inquiry was being made into the nature and reality that was initially referred to as African Traditional Religion (ATR) and later as African Religion. This inquiry progressed steadily. According to researchers and writers such as Laurenti Magesa and John Mbiti, African Religion in its own right was deemed to be in conversation with the modern world and, in Africa, with the two formally constituted missionary religions of Christianity and Islam. African Religion was understood to be serving as foundational to Africa's moral and religious values.

- **Missionary-Instituted Christianity:** By the year 2000, approximately half of Africa's one billion people had embraced Christianity. According to ecclesial statisticians and the missiological fraternity, the locus of world

Christianity had shifted to the southern hemisphere, with the vibrancy of African Christianity serving as a key element. As noted above, in addition to its religious potency, Christianity in Africa had been associated with the quest for political independence and, perhaps more indirectly, with the entry of the African populace into the modern sector of the global community. Missionary-instituted Christianity had provided significant elements of the formal institutional context within which the whole of the African ecumenical community functioned.

• **Islam in Africa:** Adherents of Islam had arrived in Africa first as refugees (received in Ethiopia by a Christian king) soon after the emergence of the Prophet Mohammed early in the seventh century. Later in the same century, Islamic forays from Egypt focused on Nubia and, in subsequent centuries, on West Africa. By the time Livingstone was traversing Africa in the early to mid-1800s, Muslim traders had found their way along Africa's west and east coasts, and had established religious and commercial networks throughout the continent. When the Western missionary movement got underway (mid-1800s) in Africa, Islam had already been present and active for a thousand years. Today Islam, like Christianity, claims the faith allegiance of approximately half of the African continent's population.

• **Secular Africa:** As in many other parts of the world, there exists in Africa a layer of modern, secularized technocrats and academics who collectively constitute a distinct segment of society. They share with their counterparts in Europe and North America a modern and, to some extent, a secular view of the world. It is this contingent of elites that provides a window onto Africa for their Western counterparts.

• **Semitic-Cushitic Africa:** Across North Africa, there remains evidence of the broad influence of the Semitic and Cushitic heritage with its origins, respectively, in the northeast and the Horn of Africa and in Sudanic Nubia along the Nile Valley. Such influence is expressed in the communities of Muslim Arabs, Falasha Jews, Orthodox/evangelical Christian Amhara, and the traditional Cushite religious traditions of the Borana, the Gabbra, and the Somalis variously penetrated by Islam and Christianity.

• **South Africans of European Descent:** In the post-apartheid period, South Africa's people of European descent—including Afrikaners of Dutch/French descent and people of British descent, the so-called colored community of European-African origins and smaller communities from many other parts of Europe and Asia form important and variously integrated segments of South Africa's heterodox population. Much of the academic prowess of South Africa continues under the control of people of European descent, with huge adjustments toward the inclusion of the African majority underway. The final shape and the eventual impact of such adjustments on the rest of the continent are slowly becoming apparent.

Jesse Mugambi has drawn comparisons between Africa and Japan, where disparate categories of a comparable nature can be identified. According to him, Japan has somehow managed to sustain its remarkably distinct religious and cultural traditions in creative and effective engagement with the rest of the world. In so doing, Japan has long enjoyed recognition as a stable, modern, non-Western, industrial world power. Mugambi covets a similar configuration for Africa's future.

Documentation

Although the definitive accounts of the ecumenical story in Africa have yet to be written, several published documents offer preliminary profiles. By far the most helpful account of the AACC's ecumenical sojourn has been captured in *Visions of Authenticity: The Assemblies of the All Africa Conference of Churches 1963-1992* by Efiong Utuk (AACC, 1997, Nairobi, Kenya). In this book, the AACC's accompanying role during the continental quest for cultural and political independence is examined through the lenses of the successive AACC General Assembly reports. Beginning with the AACC's founding in 1963, the overview concludes with an examination of the 1992 AACC General Assembly, just as signs of South Africa's shift toward majority rule were appearing on the horizon.

Other documentation on leading ecumenical personalities or major ecumenical initiatives has taken form only sporadically. An autobiography by Ghanaian Kodwo Ankrah (of Methodist origin) is focused on his various roles in the WCC, the AACC, and the Anglican Church of Uganda, telling the story of a pioneer African ecumenical personality. In the early 1980s, Agnes Aboum, a Kenyan academic, compiled a PhD dissertation on the National Council of Churches of Kenya (NCCK), focusing on the economic, development, and public advocacy roles of the council, highlighting both the deficiencies and the strengths of the council's prophetic performance. Other significant pieces of the ecumenical story in Africa have yet to be written.

Ecumenical Accountability

Within the precincts of the AACC's ecumenical family, memories regarding the moratorium debate are strong. As noted above, John Gatu of the Presbyterian Church in Kenya was a persistent advocate in the early 1970s for a moratorium on missionary funds and personnel from European and North American "mother churches" and mission societies. Like others, he was pleading for space within which young churches in Africa could hew their own paths toward ecclesial maturity. Responses to this moratorium call came in various guises. Some overseas partner churches and agencies heard the call as a rejection of their largesse, or even as a violation of the inherent mandate of Christian solidarity. Others effected institutional changes, replacing the vestiges of formal mission structures with global relational networks. Meanwhile, in the midst of this North–South discussion on appropriate ecclesial relationships, the relief, service, and development agencies of the respective Northern ecumenical agencies flourished.

Such agencies were stimulated in their growth and expansion by the UN-designated "development decades" of the 1960s and '70s, and by the related global development goals on issues such as water, food, food, shelter, and energy. By the 1990s, Africa was facing the doldrums, nursing its civil wars, and dealing with famine and growing poverty. Ecumenical service agencies, like a host of secular agencies, enjoyed a field day of institutional and programmatic expansion, quickly overshadowing any semblance of ecumenical relational parity between the African ecumenical community and its Northern counterparts.

Today, the ecumenical community in Africa is saddled with an unwieldy relational apparatus. Since the independence decade of the 1960s, National Christian Councils in Africa have been variously drawn into development or political advocacy modes. These programmatic directions have been understood and justified as a manifestation of authentic prophetic ministry by African churches. However, in that pursuit, churches and Christian Councils continued their dependency on the largesse of "donor partners" precisely when genuine ecumenical funds started to decline.

Hence the growing reliance by all concerned on what became known in the ecumenical fraternity as "back donors": North Atlantic governments that placed their overseas development funds at the disposal of ecumenical service agencies, the latter generally believed to be better positioned than official government aid agencies to apply such funds toward the genuine needs of people in Africa. In this manner, Northern ecumenical agencies served as funding channels from the "back donor" governments to their ecumenical counterparts in Africa, National Christian Councils, regional ecumenical "fellowship" structures, and the All Africa Conference of Churches.

Typically, a National Christian Council in Africa serves as an ecumenical focal point for its member churches, providing a forum for deliberation on matters of common ecclesial concern. Furthermore, such a council will be programmatically operational, fielding dozens of staff and managing a dizzying array of projects. Once a year comes reckoning time, when representatives of the various ecumenical partners-cum-donors from the North and senior representatives of a typical Christian Council converge into what are known as "round tables"—devices developed under the tutelage of the World Council of Churches for purposes of sharing resources. For all practical purposes, they function as mini-ecclesial counterparts to the forums that have brought the World Bank together with their member client states, haggling over performance reports, audited accounts, deficits/balances, and program plans for the future.

Despite emphatic protestations to the contrary, the partners-cum-donors exercised a strong hand in this "marketplace," if only because they controlled the money by means of "back donor" conditionalities that increasingly reflected the preoccupation of the Western world with "quantifiable performance indicators." Meanwhile, because of the demanding technical nature of the conditionalities, the partner/donor representatives were increasingly selected for their technical expertise rather than their ecumenical relational commitments. At best, these processes functioned as weakened facsimiles of the original ecumenical intentions that called for global fellowship and prophetic witness; at worst, they tended toward neocolonial relational postures.

Even these rather cumbersome structures could have been acknowledged as some version of functional ecumenical relationships had it not been for the fact that many Northern ecumenically constituted service agencies had themselves become operational in Africa. Here again, the requirements of back donors came into play: in order to access back donor funds, European ecumenical agencies needed to be seen by their back donors to be operational in Africa. Thus did European ecumenical agencies support projects initiated and operated by African ecumenical counterparts while initiating and implementing, quite separately, projects of their own choosing. This selective accountability was further skewed by the fact that ecumenical service agencies, as contrasted with mission or church agencies, were not intended or designed to function as the primary facilitators of ecumenical relationships between Africa and its Northern/Western church counterparts.

In fact, accountability questions did not disappear. They came increasingly under the scrutiny of more self-aware clusters of churches in Africa, both in terms of institutional and programmatic accountability, and in terms of theological accompaniment. With regard to the former, the formation of FECCLAHA—a regional ecumenical facility—served as a case in point. Churches within the ecumenical family, scattered from Eritrea to the Congo to Tanzania, were now given access to a forum where they could discuss their common ecumenical concerns and, in particular, concerns related to issues of war and peace and beyond toward the reconstruction of Africa. Subsequent to its formation in March 1999, FECCLAHA became a reference and reporting point for service activities of both African churches and overseas ecumenical agencies operational in this region.

Theological Accompaniment

Reference has already been made to the range of documentation chronicling the life of the African ecumenical community. Slightly distanced from the formal ecumenical institutional structures were the several clusters of theological reflection taking on increasing significance. One of these was the Africa chapter of the Ecumenical Association of Third World Theologians (EATWOT). Another, catering more directly for the coordination of curricula in African theological institutions, was the Conference of African Theological Institutions (CATI), which was then subdivided into regional associations across the continent.

On a more localized basis, senior theologians in Kenya took initiative to encourage theological reflection, writing, and publication. From this exercise emerged the *Christianity in Africa* series, addressing a wide range of theological ethical, social, and ecclesial concerns. Later, this series provided a service to theologians, much as the African Writers' Series of the 1950s and 1960s offered a means of expression for Africa's secular creative-writing community. Some of the theologians writing for this series were relatively young and still in formation. This forum provided an atmosphere within which theological concepts and the pressures of social and political dynamics converged to produce theological writing pertinent to emerging realities. Indeed, the *Christianity in Africa* series was hard pressed at some points to keep up with demand, with some of the books enjoying second editions.

In fascinating ways, these strains of ecumenical theological reflection served both the requirements of ecumenical accountability and the challenges posed by the ecumenical call for the reconstruction of Africa. The theological project in Africa over a period of five decades had been focused on the articulation of what became known as African Theology, a category of theological reflection viewed by some Western scholars as excessive preoccupation with African religious and cultural concerns. African theologians readily acknowledged this characterization of their work, but they saw it not as a deficiency or an unwarranted bias, but as integral to the larger African theological project. They perceived their task to be that of rendering Africa's cultural heritage, and specifically their understanding of the God of Africa, continuous and contiguous with the biblical revelation of God in the person of Jesus, the Christ.

They believed, furthermore, that a clear theological understanding of these convergences was necessary to the growth and development of the global ecumenical reality. Only when the African religious experience became as accessible and as normative as the North Atlantic Christian experience could the possibility of genuine reciprocal ecumenical relationships be realized. As conditions for higher levels of ecumenical parity were realized, greater ecumenical accountability also became a reality. Although its trajectory over the past half century has not been perfect in every respect, the general direction of the ecumenical project in Africa has been remarkable.

—*October 1999*

Resources

All Africa Conference of Churches. *Abundant Life in Jesus Christ: Report of the 6th AACC General Assembly, Oct. 25 -29, 1992*. 1994. Nairobi.

——————. International Affairs Desk. *Perspectives on Africa*. 1996. Nairobi.

Ankrah, K. E. *Development and the Church of Uganda: Mission, Myths and Metaphors*. 1999. Acton. Nairobi.

Assefa, H. and G. Wachira (eds). *Peacemaking and Democratization in Africa: Theoretical Perspectives and Church Initiatives*. 1996. All Africa Conference of Churches. Nairobi.

Bediako, K. *Christianity in Africa: The Renewal of a Non-Western Religion*. 1995. Orbis Books. Maryknoll, New York.

Getui, Mary and Emmanuel Obeng (eds). *Theology of Reconstruction: Exploratory Essays*. 1999. Acton. Nairobi.

Karamega, A. *Problems and Promises of Africa*. 1993. All Africa Conference of Churches. Nairobi.

Magesa, Laurenti. *African Religion: Moral Traditions for Abundant Life*. 1997. Orbis Books. Maryknoll, New York.

—————— and Zablon Nthamburi (eds). *Democracy and Reconciliation: A Challenge for African Christianity*. 1999. Acton. Nairobi.

Maimela, S. *Culture, Religion and Liberation*. 1994. All Africa Conference of Churches. Nairobi.

Miller, H. F. "Christian Councils in Africa: Whence? Whither?" 1996. Mennonite Central Committee. Nairobi.

_____. "African Ecumenism in a New Context." 1997. All Africa Conference of Churches. Nairobi.

_____. "Peace Talk." 1998. Review of *Transforming Violence: Linking Local and Global Peacemaking*, edited by Robert Herr and Judy Zimmerman Herr (1999, Herald Press, Scottdale, PA).

Mugambi, J. N. K. *From Liberation to Reconstruction*. 1995. East African Educational Publishers. Nairobi.

Phiri, I., K. Ross, and J. Cox (eds). *The Role of Christianity in Development Peace, and Reconstruction: Southern Africa Perspectives*. 1996. All Africa Conference of Churches. Nairobi.

Shole, K. (ed). *AACC Youth Peace Training Manual*. 1999. All Africa Conference of Churches. Nairobi.

Utuk, E. *Visions of Authenticity: The Assemblies of the All Africa Conference of Churches, 1963-1992*. 1997. All Africa Conference of Churches. Nairobi.

11
Nyerere's Gospels

The following reflections were stimulated by a nostalgia visit made to Dar es Salaam and Zanzibar, Tanzania, with Annetta in June 2010.

JULIUS KAMBARAGE NYERERE was born March 1922 in northwest Tanganyika on the east side of Lake Victoria within the Zanaki community. He died on October 14, 1999. He served as prime minister of Tanganyika from its independence on December 9, 1961, until December 9, 1962. From 1964 to 1985, he was president of the United Republic of Tanzania, a union of mainland Tanganyika and the isles of Zanzibar. Prior to entering politics, he had been employed as a schoolteacher.

The late president has been recognized as an outstanding political leader and also as an accomplished and dedicated poet, teacher, and translator. Before becoming president, he had translated two Shakespearean classics, *Julius Caesar* and *The Merchant of Venice*, into Swahili, the East African lingua franca. In his retirement he took up translation of portions of the Bible, namely the four Gospels and the book of Acts (all published by Benedictine Publications, Ndanda, Tanzania, 1996):

- *Utenzi wa Enjili: Kadiri ya Utongo wa Luka* (Gospel of Luke)
- *Utenzi wa Enjili: Kadiri ya Utongo wa Marko* (Gospel of Mark)
- *Utenzi wa Enjili: Kadiri ya Utongo wa Matayo* (Gospel of Matthew)
- *Utenzi wa Enjili: Kadiri ya Utongo wa Yohana* (Gospel of John)
- *Utenzi wa Matendo ya Mitume* (Acts of the Apostles)

It is generally recognized that the Swahili literary corpus comprises the most extensive, continuous tradition of written literature in Africa south of the Sahara Desert. Using Arabic script, Swahili has been a written language for half a millennium, with the earliest manuscripts consisting almost exclusively of poetry.

The Swahili word for a single line of poetry is *shairi*, and the plural form, *mashairi*, refers to "poetry" in general. However, the term *mashairi* may also refer to a subgenre of poems marked by the following features: they are often fairly brief in length; they may address virtually any subject; and they are much appreciated in the modern Swahili press. The lines of such poetry are usually twelve to fourteen syllables in length and divided into hemistichs (half lines of poetry), with a caesura (a pause or rest) before the final six syllables.

In Swahili antiquity, the most common form of poetry was the *utendi* (*utenzi*). This poetic subgenre was closely associated with the cultural life of Lamu, an island on Kenya's north coast. The town of Lamu functioned as an important cultural and commercial center on the Indian Ocean littoral, reaching its zenith in the eighteenth and nineteenth centuries.

In his translation undertaking, Nyerere could simply have transposed the Gospels and the book of Acts from a variety of existing Bible translations to Swahili prose. Instead, he chose to translate from the basis of New Testament Greek into the ancient but still popular poetic form of the *utendi* as the most effective means of conveying the relevance of the message of Good News to modern life in East Africa.

Tenzi (plural of *utendi/utenzi*) are narrative and didactic poems traditionally composed and intended for singing by men and women. Even today, they are popular in Swahili culture, touching on serious and informative religious teachings, recounting events of historical import, offering praise of famous people, or pronouncing warnings and exhortations.

Certain *tenzi* are considered to be epics, such as the well-known *Utendi wa Liyongo* recounting the heroic life and tragic death of Liyongo, a seventeenth- or eighteenth-century warrior of Pate, Lamu's neighbor island. Traditionally, *tenzi* comprised four-line stanzas or parts, measured by syllables. They could be composed of lines having as few as six syllable counts or as many as eleven. The most prevalent number of syllables per line was eight, making a total of thirty-two per stanza. The first three lines featured a final rhyme which varied from one stanza to the next, with the last line of the stanzas maintaining a solitary rhyme throughout the poem. A single poem could extend to a thousand or more stanzas.

Such was the poetic form apparently deemed most appropriate for President Nyerere's translation of Holy Scripture. As a literary form, it was suited to the development of long and serious themes, featuring a flexible and manipulable structure. A single line of eight syllables was long enough to express a complete idea, but short enough to allow for the formation of phrases in creating stanzas. Nevertheless, Nyerere, the poet-translator, found himself obliged to stretch the limits of both poetic form and translation accuracy. He maintained the biblical format of verses, chapters, and sections. Instead of adhering strictly to the four-line stanza pattern of the classical *tenzi*, he allowed himself the freedom to create stanzas of as few as two lines and as many as twelve lines, depending on the content and length of the verses being rendered into Swahili. He also abandoned the traditional rhyming scheme in favor of rhyming couplets. Although the majority of his stanzas feature an even number of lines, some do have an odd number. In such cases, the final syllables of the last three lines in the stanza rhyme with each other. However, the translator did adhere strictly to the pattern of eight measures per line. In the long *tenzi* tradition, a wide variety of literary devices have been deployed, challenging the composer to function within the prosodic constraints imposed by the adopted poetic form.

It can be noted, parenthetically, that President Nyerere was not the first Swahili translator to use the *tenzi* form in scripture translation. Tanzanian poet Mathias E. Mnyampala published *Utenzi wa Enjili Takatifu* (Holy Gospels) in 1963 and *Utenzi wa Zaburi* (Psalms) in 1965. These are not translations of the full text, but a retelling of the biblical story. Tanzanian poet Evaristo M. Mahimbi published *Utenzi wa Yusufu* (Epic of Joseph) in 1975.

With the publication in 1967 of the Arusha Declaration—a milestone postindependence policy document in Tanzania, Swahili became entrenched as the national and official language of Tanzania. In the region, the term "Swahili" generally refers to the people (*Mswahili/Waswahili* being the singular/plural), while *Kiswahili* refers to the language.

Up to a third of the Old Testament is written in poetic form. Without attempting to determine why biblical authors resorted to what may be identified as poetry, there is no doubt that some of the motivation for such literary rendering was emotive—that is, for the purpose of maximizing impact. Another purpose would have been to serve as an aid to memory. Mwalimu Nyerere, seeking to accomplish similar effects among his people, recognized poetry as the most effective means of reaching the people, therefore engaging his readers and listeners through the well-known and popular subgenre of *tenzi*. In this form, the message of the Bible could be recited, sung, and retained in memory. In this exercise, the poet-translator deployed religious vocabulary that had been honed over centuries within Muslim/Swahili culture into beautiful literary form, culturally familiar and acceptable to a significant portion of the readership. For students of theology and Swahili literary form, Nyerere's rendering of the Gospels and the book of Acts serves as a gold standard achievement and as a resource inviting continuing study and analysis.

Catholic Connections

Nyerere attended Makerere University in Uganda, where he studied the writings of philosophers, including the writings of Jacques Maritain. He read all of the papal encyclicals. He became the leader of the Catholic students' organization at Makerere University and organized pilgrimages to the shrines of the Uganda Martyrs. Father Richard Walsh, headmaster of St. Mary's Secondary School in Tobora, Tanganyika—where Nyerere taught for a time—became Nyerere's friend and confidant, serving as a chief fundraiser in support of Nyerere's subsequent study at the University of Edinburgh. Nyerere had at first resisted Walsh's encouragement to study in Scotland and several times had returned scholarship money collected on his behalf, fearing that he would compromise or lose his "African-ness" if he agreed to undertake studies abroad. Eventually he did accept both the scholarship funds and the opportunity to study at the University of Edinburgh. At one point during his time in Scotland, Nyerere expressed his desire to become a priest. He was discouraged from pursuing that option by Fr. Walsh, who instead advised Nyerere that he was better suited to the career of a political leader.

After studies in Scotland, Nyerere returned to Tanganyika and married Maria Waningo Gabrieli in the Nyegina Catholic Mission outstation near Musoma town on January 21, 1953. Father William Collins, a Maryknoll missioner and pastor at the Nyegina Mission, witnessed the marriage ceremony. After marriage the couple lived for a while in Butiama, Nyerere's village home. Subsequently Nyerere was recruited as a teacher to the Catholic-sponsored St. Francis Secondary School in Pugu, a community not far from Dar es Salaam.

In a June 2010 conversation with a Dutch priest in the White Fathers headquarters—lodged in one of the oldest buildings in Dar es Salaam—we were told of Nyerere's frequent visits to the headquarters building, where he used a desk—still extant but, alas, unlabeled—in the mission house, on which Nyerere drafted the constitution of TANU (Tanganyika African National Union), the political party of the day.

Mennonite Connections

Zanakiland, Nyerere's ethno-geographic home region, is located within the "catchment area" of the Mennonite Mission/Church, with its headquarters near Musoma town in the Mara Region of Tanzania. Some among his immediate family, including a stepbrother, had become members of the Mennonite Church. Joseph Butiku, the son of Nyerere's stepbrother, was one such member. During the period of our assignment in Dar es Salaam, Butiku served as a lay preacher in the small Mennonite congregation taking shape in the capital city. Butiku was married to Perusi, Annetta's childhood friend and daughter of Mennonite pastor Ezekial Maganda. In yet another tangential Mennonite link with the Nyerere story, Annetta's mother, Miriam Wenger (a widow at the time), had Maria Nyerere as one of her students in a domestic science course conducted on the Bukiroba Mennonite Church compound near Musoma town.

During the 1960s, Butiku served as the personal secretary to President Nyerere in State House. The Mennonite connection provided occasion to "listen in" on Nyerere's personal reading list, which included, at the time, Teilhard de Chardin's *The Phenomenon of Man* and the sizzling critique of Africa's newly independent elite by Rene Dumont under the title *False*

Start in Africa, the latter becoming required reading for all of Nyerere's cabinet ministers. Soon after our June 1965 arrival in Tanzania, Butiku had facilitated an appointment with President Nyerere in State House, an appointment sought by my immediate Mennonite missionary predecessor, Mahlon Hess. Thanks to acquaintances nurtured over a period of years in the Musoma/Butiama area, Hess felt the need to bid President Nyerere adieu. Additionally, according to Hess, this was an occasion to introduce me to the president of Tanzania![1] Such ready access to state power came as an incongruous but pleasant surprise to this novice, untainted until then by any direct contact with state power! Many years later, on July 21, 1999, President Nyerere attended the funeral service of Zedekiah Kisare, the first indigenous bishop of the Mennonite Church in Tanzania—conducted several dozen meters from Annetta's birthplace on the Shirati Hospital compound. President Nyerere died in December of the same year.

In June 2010 Annetta and I visited Dar es Salaam and Zanzibar for purposes almost purely nostalgic. Apart from enjoying the general atmosphere, we were curious about the status of Nyerere's legacy. How was he being remembered? To this end we visited several institutions in or near downtown Dar es Salaam and one on the eastern edge of town.

After much inquiry, we eventually found the temporary office of the Julius Nyerere Foundation, of which Joseph Butiku was the director. Much to our chagrin, we learned that he was recovering from a serious operation, confined to his home. But his helpful secretary promised to inform him of our quest to see him and even gave us his home telephone number together with permission to call him. Repeated attempts failed to rouse a response.

Some days later we made a repeat visit to the Foundation offices with a more modest but also a more specific inquiry. Is it the intent of the Foundation to collect written/published materials on the life and work of Nyerere and to publish aspects of the cumulative findings? For the answer we were ushered into the small office of a senior staff person of the Foundation. A goodly portion of the answer we were seeking—at least five inches in depth—was scattered in a totally disheveled fashion across the

---

[1] I was seconded by Eastern Mennonite Board of Missions to the Christian Council of Tanzania as Secretary for Relief and Service (1965–1971).

desk of this senior staff person. After repeating our query, the gentleman pulled several "published" volumes out from under the pile of papers and files on his desk. In the event, these volumes had just been delivered by the printers, but were being rejected because of the many typos. Apparently it had been the assumption of the Foundation staff that the process of printing would identify and correct mistakes in the original manuscript! Such was the extent of the Foundation's undertaking in publishing with regard to the life and work of the late President Nyerere.

In pursuit of another strand of Nyerere's legacy, we found ourselves aboard one of Dar es Salaam's ubiquitous public transport vehicles known as *dala-dala* (dollar-dollar), making our way to the Salvation Army conference and training compound located on the eastern edge of the city. Upon arrival in Tanzania in 1965, we had spent our first several weeks of orientation and overlap time with our predecessors on this compound.

At that time the accommodation for visitors consisted of very basic, small thatched-roofed structures. On this nostalgia visit, we found the pied crows still there with their calls and responses and the palm trees still swaying in the wind. But the thatched roofs had been replaced with more permanent corrugated materials.

During our stay in the 1960s, we had become intrigued by another guest at the Salvation Army center. She was a British woman by the name of Joan Wicken, serving at the time, and for many subsequent years, as Nyerere's intellectual/ideological sparring partner and as his resident in-house researcher/compiler/writer. She was responsible for "pulling together" virtually all of Nyerere's formal reflections/writings and seeing them through to publication. Wicken travelled from the Salvation Army compound to State House every day on her little red 50 cc Vespa scooter, rejecting repeated offers from Nyerere for transport by Mercedes limo.

When we asked the administrator of the Salvation Army compound to show us the hut in which Wicken had lived, he readily obliged. We were astonished, again, by the smallness of the structure, but also by the fact that there was no visible indication that Wicken had once lived there. In the absence of any kind of identifying or memorial placard, will the next administrator remember the erstwhile presence on the compound of the remarkable personality that was Joan Wicken?

Our third port of call was the Julius Nyerere Memorial Academy, known in the 1960s as Kivukoni College, with a mandate then to promote and train select Tanzanians toward an ethos of *Ujamaa* (familyhood), Nyerere's national ideology. From downtown Dar es Salaam, the Academy is reached by means of a perfunctory ferry ride to the eastern shore of Dar es Salaam's magnificent harbor and then a short walk.

After indicating the nature of our quest, we were ushered into the office of the principal, Dr. John Magotti. We learned quickly that Magotti had attended Musoma Alliance Secondary School, where one of his teachers had been our friend Maynard Kurtz, seconded to the institution by the Mennonite Mission. We also learned that Dr. Magotti was a member of the Jita community from Mugango, the village where Annetta spent some portion of her childhood and where she picked up smatterings of the Jita language. So there followed some easy Jita banter between Annetta and Magotti.

When we asked how Nyerere's legacy was being served by the Academy, we were introduced to the librarian. He dutifully showed us a huge cardboard box containing a collection of Nyerere's writings and materials about Nyerere, published by a variety of authors, but nothing published by the Academy. When we inquired, neither the librarian nor Dr. Magotti had heard of Nyerere's translation of the Gospels and Acts. In a follow-up email, we thanked Director Magotti for the generous reception, but took the occasion to highlight the lacuna regarding Nyerere's Gospels. Several days later, Magotti sent us an email indicating that the librarian had been dispatched to the St. Joseph Bookshop to purchase copies of Nyerere's translations of the Gospels and the Acts of the Apostles. With this gesture, we concluded that at least one segment of our journey of nostalgia had proven fruitful.

—*June 2010, Nairobi, Kenya*

Sources

The above technical details regarding Nyerere's translation are drawn from a paper presented by Phil Noss and Peter Renju, translation consultants in East Africa, at the Conference on Bible Translation sponsored by the Graduate Institute of Applied Linguistics, Summer Institute of Linguistics International, Dallas, Texas, October 19–21, 2003.

Earlier treatments of this topic appeared as "The *Tenzi* of Mwalimu Nyerere: Scripture Translation in Poetic Form" by Philip A. Noss and Peter M. Renju in Ernst M. Wendland and Jean-Claude Loba-Mkole (eds), *Biblical Texts and African Audiences* (2004, Acton Publishers, Nairobi) and "Scripture Translation in Poetic Form: The *Tenzi* of Mwalimu Nyerere" by Phil Noss and Peter Renju in Simon Crisp and Jan de Waard (eds), *Text, Theology and Translation* (2004, United Bible Societies).

Dar Days: The Early Years in Tanzania by Charles Swift (2002, University Press of America).

12
The Quest for an Open Sudan

Book Review of *Seeking an Open Society: Inter-Faith Relations and Dialogue in Sudan Today*

An important unresolved debate in Sudan today is concerned with the relationship between religion and state. In Sudan, Islam is the dominant religion, while Christianity constitutes a significant religious minority. Within the government of Sudan, there is strong support for rule by means of Islamic law (sharia). During past decades, even centuries, the debate has been consistently intense. The rise and reign of the messianic Mahdi (the "sent one") and his immediate successor in the 1880s serves as an historic reference point for governance based on the sharia. Then as now, some portion of that debate has been situated within the Muslim-Christian matrix.

But it was not always so. Strange as it may seem, Christianity was established in Sudan well before the advent of Islam. From approximately AD 500 to AD 1400, Christianity flourished along the Nile Valley, northward from the present capital city of Khartoum to the border with Egypt. It took shape within the three Christian kingdoms of Nobatia, Makuria, and Alodia, archaeological artifacts of which are prominently displayed in Khartoum's National Museum. The medieval history of Christianity in Sudan has been extensively recorded (Vantini 1981) and attracts continued research. A growing awareness of this heritage has emboldened modern Sudanese Christians to claim their rightful place in the religious history of Sudan, and thus in the ongoing, but somewhat strained, Muslim-Christian dialogue.

Sudan is a complex country. It straddles the Afro-Arab divide within northern and central Africa. Its 26 million people represent nineteen major ethnic groups and speak some 115 languages, with Arabic serving as the national language, several versions of which are spoken throughout the country. Because of Sudan's Anglo-Egyptian colonial history, English is also widely spoken. Southern Sudanese, many of whom are Christians, note that the largest portion of the peoples of Sudan are of African descent, while Northern Sudanese, especially those of Arab descent and adherents of the Muslim faith, emphasize the apparent reality that people of the Islamic faith comprise the largest portion of the Sudanese people. Southerners speak easily of the commonality of Sudan's African peoples, while Arab Northerners speak of the benevolent nature of Arab-Muslim hegemony.

These contentious factors fuel the current civil war. Except for a respite from 1972 to 1983, Sudan has been engaged in civil war since its independence from Britain in 1956. The Addis Ababa Peace Accord of 1972 brought a seventeen-year war to an end. But differences between the Khartoum government and Southern dissidents rekindled the civil war in 1983, which continues to the present. Currently, international news media focus on the war because of the disastrous famine which has claimed the lives of many thousands of Southern Sudanese.

It is against this backdrop that this slender volume on Christianity in Sudan takes on significance. The book is one of a series produced from papers presented at a conference convened in Nairobi, Kenya, in 1997 under the theme "The Church in Sudan: Its Impact Past, Present, and Future." Stuart Brown, the editor of the book, serves as the director of the Project on Muslim Christian Relations (PROCMURA), an ecumenical Christian initiative in Africa mandated to foster dialogue between Muslims and Christians. In his work, Dr. Brown has consistently emphasized the commonalties that characterize the "Abrahamic faith traditions" (Judaism, Christianity, and Islam), or "people of the book" as they are referred to in the Quran. In an editorial note, Brown appeals to those common values.

One of the contributing writers, Gerhard Lichtenthaler, examines the "National Issues, Political Styles and Islamic Responses" of Sudan by offering a well-researched case study of Mahmud Muhammad Taha, the "liberal" Sufi-oriented leader of the Republican Brothers. For his relatively liberal interpretation of Islam, including an insistence on the total equality of women, Taha was executed at age seventy-six by the Sudan government on January 18, 1985. Taha, together with fellow intellectuals, had formed the Republican Party in 1945 as an alternative to other political parties, which were criticized by Taha for having compromised with the colonial powers. Taha represented but one of numerous Islamic traditions in Sudan.

Islam in Sudan is not hierarchically structured. Because of its decentralized character and its common mystic, pietistic Sufi traditions, Islam in Sudan has been preoccupied with questions of authority, proper governance, and, more specifically, with the role of sharia or Islamic law in modern governance systems. It could be argued that the debate on these issues within Sudan's Islamic community were in fact more intense than the rather secondary tensions between Christians and Muslims.

In his contribution to the book, the Rev. Ezekiel Kujok, former general secretary of the Sudan Council of Churches, traced in considerable detail the formation of official Muslim-Christian dialogue in Sudan, a process in which he participated from its inception. These efforts resulted in two international conferences, the first the Conference on Religions in Sudan, held in 1993; the second the Inter-Religious Dialogue Conference, held in 1994. These conferences coincided with the formation of an Inter-Religious Dialogue Association, intended to serve as the official vehicle in Sudan for fostering inter-faith dialogue, including Muslim-Christian discussion, as well as engagement with traditional religion.[1]

Both conferences were attended by European Muslims from countries such as Britain, Sweden, Germany, and Bosnia, and Middle Eastern countries such as Syria, Lebanon, and Egypt. I attended on behalf of the general secretary of the All Africa Conference of Churches. Staged as official and relatively lavish events, those conferences were perceived by Southern Christians as a way of polishing Sudan's rather tarnished international religious image at the expense of fostering genuine dialogue between Christians and Muslims within the country. Interestingly, Middle Eastern Christians in attendance at the conferences seemed to enjoy greater sociocultural affinity with Northern Sudanese Muslims than with Southern Sudanese Christians; the latter would claim to be victims of the negative

---

1 During the 1993 conference, the famous Southern Sudanese writer Taban Lo Liyong, an avowed practitioner of traditional religion, presented a paper entitled "Indigenous Religion in Three West African Societies."

impact of cultural, political, and historic dynamics within Sudan, realities not easily ignored or readily resolved.

Additionally, the conferences highlighted markedly contrasting assumptions with regard to religious dialogue; Northern Sudanese presenters at the conferences made virtually no distinction between the expectations of the government and the perceived requirements of Islamic jurisprudence. Additionally, representatives of the Khartoum government had identified Sudan with a revivalist Islam, "heralding a new transition in the Islamic world, one which is bound to have impact on the world at large. We [Sudanese] take pride in being in the forefront of a sweeping revivalist movement in the world of Islam (Al-Atabani 1994).

For pragmatic and obvious political reasons, Sudanese Christians, including Southern political dissidents, were insisting on the separation of religion and state. Official peace talks between the rebel South Sudan Peoples' Liberation Movement (SPLM) and the government of Sudan had reached an impasse precisely on this issue. However, any cursory reading of history quickly demonstrated that the advent of Christianity in Africa was profoundly linked to the imperial designs of the colonial state. (In the aforementioned ancient kingdoms of Sudan, it may be recalled, Christianity functioned as a state religion.) In the context of these conferences, Christians worked on the assumption that religious dialogue must take place among competent theologians or committed practitioners from the respective religious communities, thus maintaining the avowed commitment to the separation of religion and state.

In another remarkable article, Michael Parker recounted the strange saga of the conversion of a Sudanese family from Islamic to Christian faith. For readers acquainted with clear-cut conversions as fostered by Western missionary convention, this conversion story is riddled with visions, mystery, and the charisma of a powerful head of an extended family. In many respects, this conversion story is more easily understood in the context of Sudan's mystic Sufi tradition. In a personal encounter with the Roman Catholic priest who was well acquainted with the family, the writer was told that the faith journey of this remarkable family was still unfolding and was not yet recognizable as a stable Christian expression, though it was nevertheless recognized as a profound expression of Sudanese spirituality.

Given the unique history of Sudan, it was exceedingly difficult for the outsider to understand the complex attendant dynamics. In a well-argued treatise, a Sudanese writer has insisted that the problems of Sudan can be attributed to "conflicting identities," including religious identities: "Religion in the Sudanese political context is no longer a matter of personal ethics, piety, spirituality or morality; but a lethal weapon in the power struggle" (Deng 1995). Strong words. Some Western observers of Sudan's politicians tended to agree. They perceived the leadership of Dr. Hassan al-Turabi in Sudan's ruling National Islamic Front as a distortion of both religion and politics. On the other hand, the recent US missile attack on a Khartoum factory (in retaliation for the bombing of the US embassy in Nairobi) does nothing to mollify what is perceived, rightly or wrongly, to be militant Islam in Sudan. The call for an open society in Sudan must surely be extended to include a call for an open world in which adherents of religions engage in dialogue and in which politicians deploy peaceful instruments to resolve their differences.

In the quest for an "open society" in Sudan, Muslim-Christian dialogue was not assumed to constitute a process sufficient to achieve the peace of the land, but it was intended to provide an important entry point toward that end. Happily, this book provided a basis for some optimism and evidence of considerable effort, however plodding, in the direction of interfaith understanding, a process that in Sudan always touched on intercultural, interracial, interregional, and interparty elements as well.

One can only concur with the concluding paragraph by the editor: "Patience and perseverance are not abstract qualities but spiritual disciplines which [can be squandered] at our peril. Africa is at the forefront of the worldwide state of Christian-Muslim relations and Sudan is in the spotlight."

"If they incline to peace, incline yourself to it as well and trust in God, for he is all-hearing and all-knowing." —Quran 8:6

"If it is possible, so far as it depends on you, live peaceably with all men." —Romans 12:18

—August 1998, Nairobi, Kenya

Published in *Wajibu* magazine, Vol. 13. No. 3, 1998.

Resources

Al-Atabani, Dr. Ghazi Salahuddin. "Sudan's Experience in Religious Tolerance." Presentation at the October 1994 Conference on Inter-Religious Dialogue. [Al-Atabani was State Minister for Political Affairs.]

Brown, Stuart E. (Editor). *Seeking an Open Society: Inter-Faith Relations and Dialogue in Sudan Today.* 1997. Faith in Sudan Series No. 2. Paulines Publications Africa. Nairobi.

Deng, Francis M. *War of Visions: Conflict of Identities in the Sudan.* 1995. The Brookings Institution. Washington, D.C.

Vantini, Giovanni. *Christianity in the Sudan.* 1981. Collegio delle Missioni Africane. Italy.

13
An Encounter with *Fan into Flame* by John G. Gatu

ON DECEMBER 15, 2016, I attended a book launch in the old chapel of St. Andrew's Presbyterian Church in Nairobi. The book being celebrated was *Fan into Flame* by ninety-two-year-old Rev. Dr. John G. Gatu. A majority of those attending the event were associated with the Presbyterian Church of East Africa (PCEA). I was the only expatriate "missionary type" in attendance throughout the proceedings; a French-Canadian Catholic priest came late and left early. Several close Kenyan friends were in attendance, as were several people known for their roles in church-related activities. John Gatu was present, sitting in his wheelchair, accompanied by members of his family.

The order of service consisted of the Presbyterian liturgy with some deference to the East African Revival tradition, of which Rev. Gatu was an ardent lifelong adherent. Surprisingly, most of the commentary throughout the event consisted of relatively lightweight banter, with only the most cursory reference to the actual content of the book being launched. By far the most serious reflection was offered by the guest of honor, Rev. Dr. Samuel Kobia.

Kobia hails from the Meru ethnic community rooted in the northeast side of Mt. Kenya, where the Methodist Church has long been dominant. His trajectory through the various layers of denominational and ecumenical engagement at local, national, and international levels, and latterly within government officialdom, had been quite extraordinary, facilitated and encouraged along the way by his friend and mentor John Gatu. Ordained originally to Christian ministry in the Methodist Church, Kobia was subsequently appointed as General Secretary of the National Council of Churches of Kenya (NCCK), and some years later as General Secretary of the World Council of Churches (WCC), followed by a stint as the ecumenical envoy (appointed by the WCC and the All Africa Conference of Churches (AACC) to Sudan and to the world's youngest nation, South Sudan, which gained its independence in 2011. Then followed appointments to a position within a Kenyan governmental judiciary committee and a position in the office of the president of Kenya as an advisor on matters of peace and reconciliation.

Six years after the achievement of Kenya's national independence in 1961, President Jomo Kenyatta had publicly announced the first general elections. Concomitantly and clandestinely, he had also initiated an "oathing" exercise among his own ethnic Gikuyu people in an effort to ensure that Kenya's presidency would be retained by "the House of Mumbi" (the Gikuyu people) in perpetuity. In that context, John Gatu, together with several fellow clergymen, had taken it upon themselves to challenge and rebuke President Kenyatta for what they considered to be a negative and destructive initiative. In his speech, Kobia made only the slightest reference to the oathing dramatics, following other speakers who had completely avoided any reference to them. This silence during the book launch regarding this crucial initiative by Gatu and colleagues was deafening.

Immediately following the book launch, tea and pastries were on offer. Except for an exchange of greetings and pleasantries with several close Kenyan friends, there was no interaction with any of the other persons present. During the launch proceedings, several speakers had referred to the roles of missionaries within the Presbyterian Church and within the wider Kenyan church community. While the positive contributions of some missionaries had been noted, critiques of their negative influence seemed to dominate. Was I being excessively sensitive as the lone "missionary type" present for the occasion? Were participants other than my friends deliberately avoiding even eye contact during teatime? These were fascinating moments, and a poignant finale to the book launch.

Very soon after the book launch, *The Standard* newspaper of Nairobi carried a front-page article on Gatu's book, zeroing in on the most sensitive chapter in his book, detailing President Jomo Kenyatta's 1969 oathing initiative and Gatu's challenge to that initiative. Shortly after the publicity in *The Standard*, an envoy from State House (where Jomo Kenyatta's son Uhuru was now serving as Kenya's president) was dispatched to Gatu's son with a firm rebuke for including and exposing in the new book the sensitive record of the 1969 oathing episode. The carefully crafted texts that Gatu and fellow clergy had delivered to President Jomo Kenyatta, registering their abhorrence of the oathing exercise, were being made public and attracting official government reaction for the first time since the 1969 episode. On January 8, 2017, the Rev. Canon Francis Omondi, a staff member of the Anglican All Saints Cathedral in Nairobi, had an article of his published in the politically left-of-center newspaper, *The Star*, entitled "Why Uhuru Must Free Kenya from His Father's Oathing." Soon after the publication of the article, Canon Omondi was being trailed by Kenya's secret service and pointedly confronted and rebuked for his article.

During the previous decade or more, Annetta and I had been meeting every Saturday morning with two or three Kenyan professor friends. We discussed current events; we exchanged books of mutual interest; we enlarged our common precincts by inviting special guests as resource people; and, occasionally, we took on the planning for and execution of some project. Significant aspects of my book *The Murang'a Murals* had been conceived, nurtured, and propagated during our Saturday-morning meetings.

When *Fan into Flame* was launched on December 15, 2016, Professor Kabiru Kinyanjui from our Saturday morning group and I were present. Also present was Prof. Fr. Lawrence Njoroge, Kinyanjui's longtime friend. For the following Saturday-morning meeting, Njoroge was invited to help us digest the Gatu book. In subsequent Saturday coffee sessions, it was agreed that our group would plan for a public forum focused on the Gatu book to which select professors and students from universities would be invited. Moran Publishers agreed to provide the necessary funds for the planned seminar.

Arrangements were made with the AACC for the use of its José Chipenda Conference Hall. In the meantime, our little group became deeply engaged in detailed planning for a seminar program, assembling a list of people to be invited, with special focus on university professors and students. More easily than might have been expected, the several bits of the seminar came together, culminating in a remarkably successful event on March 1, 2017. Both the formal presentations and the ensuing plenary discussion were of notable quality and of great interest. Audience discussion could have continued well beyond the allotted program time.

In the wake of the intense planning and implementation exercises related to the Gatu book, it was deemed appropriate that our organizing committee allocate space and time for relaxation and recovery. For this purpose, we were invited to Njoroge's rural ancestral home on Saturday, March 4, where we were graciously hosted by himself and his ninety-year-old mother. From Nairobi, located at about 5,500 feet above sea level, the road trip to the small town of Limuru involved a rather dramatic ascent to the eastern lip of the Great Rift Valley.

Immediately upon entry into Limuru town, one negotiated a sharp right turn leading past a densely packed series of roadside shops, and thence onto an ascending grade into a lush green expanse of tea estates. The Njoroge farm is situated amid tea estates on a gentle slope at 7,200 feet above sea level, offering crisp fresh air in contrast to Nairobi's exhaust-laden atmosphere and a wall-to-wall vista of lush tea plantations to the east.

Before sitting down to a feast of fish, roasted goat, rice, beef stew with vegetables, and an assortment of fruits, we were led by Njoroge on a tour of the several acres that had been bequeathed to him by his late father. We were astonished to learn that Njoroge had planted more than five thousand indigenous highland forest trees, including 122 varieties. Most impressive was the well-ordered planting pattern and the fact that Njoroge could identify respective tree species by their Latin botanical designations, citing as his source a well-thumbed reference book assembled by an accomplished Kenyan botanist.

Many years earlier, Njoroge's father had planted wattle trees on the farm, the bark of which had found a ready market in a nearby factory. Wattle bark contains a tannin used in tanning leather. Additional income had been realized from the sale of residual wattle-tree firewood. Eventually, the wattle-processing factory had closed down, at which point senior Njoroge switched to the planting of eucalyptus trees, a fast-growing variety with origins in Australia, yielding readily saleable timber products.

Immediately upon taking possession of his portion of the family's ancestral land, Njoroge had uprooted and removed all the eucalyptus trees. He then began his multiyear planting cycle of indigenous highland forest varieties. Within three years after replacing the eucalyptus with indigenous trees, he observed that several streams that had earlier disappeared because of the thirsty eucalyptus trees were flowing again, much to his satisfaction.

What was the purpose of this remarkable one-man campaign to reconstitute a highland forest regime? Njoroge seemed to derive great satisfaction from the rightness of planting indigenous tree varieties compatible in every way with the altitude, the quality of the land, and the related scope for the judicious interplanting of food crops. And what was the long-term value of this effort? Perhaps future accounting systems would recognize the multilayered values of highland forest trees and the concomitant interplanting of basic food crops such as maize, beans, and a variety of greens. After teatime, with a delightful array of pastries and boiled taro root, we traipsed out to our hostess's garden plot, where a tightly strung string indicated a line along which we were being invited to plant a variety of highland forest tree seedlings. We took turns embedding the seedlings into the lush soil, a most satisfying finale to an amazing afternoon.

Soon after these refreshing exercises, our coffee group urged each of the presenters at the March 1 seminar on the Gatu book to send us written versions of their oral presentations. In addition to the seminar papers, we were able to obtain, with the consent of all concerned, the keynote speech presented by the Rev. Sam Kobia at the launch of Gatu's book on December 15, 2016. Within weeks, papers were received, immediately edited, then double-checked with presenters to ensure satisfaction all around. These were then sent to my son Edward for formatting into a fifty-eight-page document.

On Thursday, May 11, 2017, the Rev. John Gatu passed away. On Monday May 15, after a weekend consultation with his superiors, Timothy Muita sent the document to all the seminar participants. In the meantime, it was announced that the funeral service for John Gatu was to be held in the Presbyterian Church near the Nairobi suburb of Karen on May 19.

Early on the morning of May 19, I made my way to Karen via the village of Kikuyu, and thence onto the southern bypass road. In Karen, I enjoyed a leisurely cup of coffee and then drove to the small Presbyterian Church where the funeral was to be held.

Hundreds of mourners had arrived well before the ten a.m. service. They were assembling in a huge tent with a seating capacity for thousands. To the right of the entrance to the tent, Moran Publishers had set up a small bookselling kiosk. One of the young ladies in charge of the kiosk recognized and greeted me as one of the organizers of the March 1 seminar on Gatu's book.

After much shuffling and arranging, the long lines of church dignitaries were seated in the designated places, some near the front of the vast numbers of mourners, with senior representatives of diverse church agencies and ecumenical organizations on the raised dais.

Apart from the large numbers of mourners in attendance—at least three thousand—aspects of the service itself were notable. Adherents of the East Africa Revival were conspicuous by their numbers and by the enthusiastic singing of the movement's signature songs, including "Kutendereza Yesu" ("Rejoice in Jesus"). Equally notable was the presence of representatives from diverse denominations and ecumenical organizations, including the NCCK and AACC, recognition of Gatu's far-flung ecumenical engagements. Impressive as well was the presence of a large number of men introduced as members of the Presbyterian Men's Fellowship that Gatu had initiated.

Several of the prominent mourners referred to Gatu's much-publicized mantra, "Let missionaries go home and financial support from Western churches be suspended for five years to allow for growth of self-reliance among Kenyan churches," as a quest for and the achievement of "dignity." Within the Presbyterian Church in Kenya, the consequent widely adopted slogan had become "*jitegemea*" (self-reliance). When passing by the entrance of the nearby Presbyterian worship center, I noted the word *jitegemea* embedded in the terrazzo entrance patio—Gatu's mantra cast in stone.

Approximately half an hour after the service had begun, President Uhuru Kenyatta made his entry. Earlier, his mother, Mama Ngina, had arrived and taken a seat with the assembled mourners. Her presence was recognized by the emcee: she rose to her feet and waved a greeting to the vast audience. At one point during the service, President Uhuru Kenyatta was invited to offer his remarks. He did so in well-modulated tones, recalling the many visits that Gatu in his pastoral role had made to the Kenyatta home during the president's childhood years. At the conclusion of his remarks, President Kenyatta was presented with a copy of *Fan into Flame*. At no time during the service was any mention made of Gatu's courageous anti-oathing challenge to President Jomo Kenyatta in 1969 on the eve of the first general elections in independent Kenya.

There followed what seemed like an endless series of introductions of church dignitaries, the purpose of which rather eluded my ready understanding. I left the service before its formal conclusion with impressions sufficient to dominate my thoughts for a long time. A great man, John G. Gatu, had come into our lives. He had made huge contributions to many aspects of church and community life in Africa, and had left us with remarkable memories and enormous appreciation for a life well lived.

—*May 2017*

14
Making Peace with the Future: Perspectives on the Relief-Development Mix

IN 1913, there was a Sahelian drought as severe as the one witnessed by the world in the 1970s. But there were differences. The world's news network was much less developed in 1913. There was no United Nations. There were few relief organizations featuring worldwide monitoring or response ability. Nor was the notion of "development" assumed in common international parlance.

A combination of world wars, eco-sociopolitical upheaval, and a general technological explosion—conspicuously affecting international travel—changed the world and in some sense made modern disasters possible. It could be argued that the 1913 drought was not a disaster of significant dimensions, simply because it did not attract world attention. The Bolshevik Revolution of 1917 in Czarist Russia was one of the early, modern disasters that did attract international attention.

The organization I represent, the Mennonite Central Committee (MCC), was born in 1920, during the "fallout" period of the 1917 Russian upheaval. During the previous 150 years, Russia had become home for thousands of Mennonites who had migrated from what is now Poland and, earlier, from the Netherlands. It was a move made at the invitation of Czarina Catherine the Great of Russia. Mennonites transformed the Ukraine into a breadbasket, and in the process became what ideologues of the Bolshevik Revolution referred to as kulaks—rich exploiters. Mennonites who lost their farms and their wealth because of the Revolution subsequently sought and received aid from coreligionist Mennonites in the

United States and Canada. MCC was created amid these dynamics. Ever since, MCC has been ready to respond to disasters.

The services of MCC and dozens of other American relief organizations were called upon after the devastation wreaked on Europe by World War II. Subsequent upheavals created by wars, floods, and earthquakes mobilized existing relief agencies and usually spawned new ones. In short, natural and sociopolitical disasters provided fertile settings for the birth and activity of relief agencies. The pattern has continued apace in situations across the world, too numerous to mention.

Another major stimulant to the birth of voluntary agency activity emerged under the rubric of development. "Development" was a concept coined by US president Harry Truman in the wake of World War II during a period broadly coinciding with the birth in 1948 of the United Nations Organization—a sequel to the League of Nations. By the late 1950s and early 1960s, political independence was sweeping across countries around the world that had long been under the tutelage of European colonial rule. In that context, the 1960s were designated by the UN as the First Development Decade. This was characterized by frenetic pursuit of reconstruction in Europe, by rendering former colonies into nation-states, by identifying globally appropriate standards of living, and generally by the dynamic of modernity facilitated by a process known as development. As a change process, development was hugely informed by technology and the related cultural accruements from the industrialized West. It followed that development activity was understood as a transfer of technique, technology, expertise, and capital, as well as a transfer of commensurate consumer tastes.

The decade of the 1970s brought into focus radical new perspectives. Aspirations of the 1960s had pushed the change capacity of the world into strange new encounters with the planet's finitude. On the one hand, there was the problem of physically and logistically maintaining the pace of development—deploying expertise, mobilizing capital, and moving the requisite technologies into place. On the other hand, there was the growing awareness of the planet's limitations—an understanding that the resources of the world available to the development process were in fact finite. This intuition was given formal status in the 1972 United Nations Conference on the Human Environment, convened in Stockholm, Sweden, and referred to since as "Stockholm." In many ways, Stockholm marked the end of innocence for development's change agents. It also brought into focus the relationship between modern disasters and the attendant responses—that is, conventional relief activity—on the one hand, and development as one source of recurring disaster, on the other.

In the ten-year period after Stockholm, the United Nations organized eighteen global conferences on subjects that clearly indicated the close and growing relationship between globally pursued development activity and the constraints that were triggering attendant relief responses. A list of those conferences will be remembered by many, although it may be forgotten by most that all eighteen conferences were convened within a single decade. As a collectivity, they triggered an explosion of global awareness with few parallels in the history of the planet.

It goes without saying that these conferences drew on insights from the First Development Decade. But credit must also be given to that creative band of philosophers, prophets, seers, scientists, and laypeople of all sorts who had long entertained doubts about the nature and direction of the world's change process. Those conferences formalized latent intuitions and brought them to world attention.

Many of the conferences birthed organizational structures designed to further analyze the problems and possibilities identified, and to establish follow-up institutions and implementing processes. The establishment of those global implementing and monitoring entities materialized in rapid-fire succession, until it suddenly became obvious that the world community of nations possessed neither the will nor the capacity to respond technically and politically to many of the problems that had arisen on a global scale. Significantly, in that context, the United Nations Conference on New and Renewable Sources of Energy (Nairobi, 1981) did not birth a typical follow-up UN "secretariat."

The Second Development Decade brought us face to face with all manner of limitations. The series of conferences demonstrated that the development patterns as well as the related aspirations could not possibly be met by deploying existing technologies and change models...this because current change models were ecologically and in many other ways considered to be unacceptably costly!

This more or less circuitous route of perceptions and understandings has been reflected in the activities of the agencies. Agencies that in the post–World War II period had established a relief capacity and subsequently a development capacity, were now again equipping themselves for relief activity. From the late 1940s to the late 1970s, the agencies came full circle. One could be forgiven for suspecting that there may be a cause-and-effect relationship between the various aspects of this activity cycle. Could it be that current sociopolitical disasters are at least in part explicable as results of the development explosion? Could it be that development has become the birthplace of new disasters?

As an aside, it is astonishing that disaster response has over the four-decade period hardly changed at all. In each new situation, agencies rush in and stake out their territory, and unless there is the heavy coordinating hand of the host government or coordination from one of the UN agencies, they struggle only slowly, if at all, toward coordination of effort. Already in the late 1940s there was discussion in the context of the International Council of Voluntary Agencies to pre-structure disaster response, parceling out predetermined roles for the several agencies. Happily, there is some movement in the right direction on coordination in the relief stages, although it is still in a "primitive" phase. But as subsequent activity shifts from relief toward development, coordination diminishes. Is this preparation of some kind for the next disaster?

The history of disaster and disaster response (or relief) is much more complex than suggested in this brief outline. An observer is free to dispute and discuss the alleged relationships between relief, development, and renewed disaster. As in all other enterprises, changes are underway, however imperceptible. With the benefit of hindsight, it would seem that in the future, relief and development agencies would have the possibility and the responsibility of choosing—at least to a limited extent—the nature of the disasters that might befall the world. To a limited extent, choices for a peaceful or a disruptive future can be made.

The reason for this shift and for the change possibility has to do with the fact that the development or change models of the world are themselves changing. An obvious example comes to mind: since the World Health Organization Conference in the USSR in 1978, much of the world community has accepted a new definition of health and, more particularly, a new standard of health care. The Western model of health care has in part been traded in for a health care pattern informed heavily by a non-Western country, in this case, China.

The examples are multiplying. The change model guiding the world during the past two decades has for the most part emerged from technology, accompanied by a belief in the technical fix: if a sufficient quantity of dollars and a sufficient volume of expertise are thrown at a problem, it will either go away or it will be solved.

In the meantime, it has been found, of course, that the technical fix at best creates political dependencies and at worst creates new, unmanageable problems. There is, for example, considerable evidence that the Sahelian catastrophe of the 1970s was caused by an inappropriate degree of development. Too many wells had allowed for the existence of too much livestock. The "normal" drought cycle did its work, efficiently and devastatingly. In other words, the strength of the Sahelian disaster was to a degree determined when the change model—including the wells and the attendant machinery and organization—was chosen.

The new definition of health already alludes to new change resources. By choosing a primary health care model, the choice toward a greater reliance on the traditional medical wisdom of people has been made.

One of the greatest continuing challenges for relief and development agencies in Africa has to do with the Sahelian zone. It is clear, on the one hand, that the lifestyle of pastoral peoples is changing rapidly, partly because of semi-settlement, partly because of lower infant mortality rates and thus population increases, and partly for other reasons. This change becomes evident in years when the rainfall is "normal." These days, the pastoral peoples do really well only in abnormally "good" years.

Over the past one-and-a-half decades, the development options for the pastoral peoples have been suggested by relief models. In northern Kenya, for example, millions of shillings were spent in establishing irrigation schemes, which from the beginning were seen as relief measures. They were not designed for economic or social viability and, as might be expected, they have proven unviable. But they have managed in the interim to give the impression in many quarters that development schemes in the arid zones require high-tech and high-level expertise to design schemes that feed thirsty crops for distant, complex markets. Thus have relief and development efforts combined to lead pastoral peoples into unviable options, which from time to time require relief responses in increasingly large quantities.

Both relief and development responses deserve better than this. Here are a few suggestions:

- It must be assumed that technology or the technical fix, alone, may provide necessary but not sufficient tools for either relief or development activity.
- By far the greatest resources, particularly for any activity in the so-called development arena, are to be found in many forms of local (often traditional) wisdom within a variety of local organizations and structures.
- For both relief and development activities, it would seem imperative to identify and create approaches to solutions by deliberately investing in local structures with a view to strengthening capacity to respond to local needs with local resources.

It is striking that precisely at a time when the modern sector in Uganda is in disarray, local, traditional food is in good supply. Is the necessary corollary that when the modern sector and the cash crops are again in place that Uganda will then, like other more "stable" nations, need to do constant battle with food deficits?

Another example from the arid Sahelian zone: Somalia is home to one-third of the world's camels. These, together with other livestock, have for many years provided the largest portion of the country's foreign exchange. So far, little has been done to "rationalize" the country's most common natural resource. Would it not be wise for a voluntary agency or a collectivity of agencies to invest in such an enterprise, thus enlarging, diversifying, and rendering more useful the most abundant of the local resources?

Here's another example, this one from Kenya. A project by the staff of the National Council of Churches of Kenya on the lower Tana River engaged local rice farmers in an exercise that examined, upgraded, and recycled the best of local rice-cultivation practices. The initial result: more confidence among farmers with regard to their own knowledge; the maintenance of a large number of varieties, and thus a protection against weather and disease; and resilient options for the long-term regional planners.

Examples abound. The principle is clear: acknowledgment of and investment in local people and their skills are among the first steps toward the prevention of recurring food shortages and development patterns that produce their own upheavals.

—November 1981

15
Testing Perceptions on the Gulf War

IN THE CONTEXT of the Gulf War, partner agencies requested the All Africa Conference of Churches (AACC) to share insights, information, or actions generated by churches in Africa. In response, a quick telephone survey of major church and ecumenical offices in Nairobi was carried out. With the exception of the Kenya Catholic Secretariat and the bishop of the Methodist Church in Kenya, both of whom had voiced concerns prior to the outbreak of the hostilities, no response action had been generated, nor had any statements been made. From AMECEA—the regional Catholic office—there was an indication that the subject would probably arise during a forthcoming meeting of bishops from the region, but the secretariat would not speculate on the nature of possible action or comment.

Informal Discussion

Partly in response to the inquiry from concerned friends of the AACC, representatives from a variety of organizations were invited to the AACC in the wake of the war for an afternoon of reflection and sharing of concerns regarding the Gulf War. In the event, ten people responded to the invitation. Even though this proved to be an extremely low-key encounter, the ensuing discussion was wide-ranging and analytical.

Concern was expressed about perceived aggression in the current conflict. While conceding that President Hussein of Iraq had engaged in provocative acts, it was felt by some participants that the primary responsibility for armed hostilities lay on the side of the Western allies. Other participants were of the opinion that any blaming for the initial aggression was beside the point; all parties involved had acted aggressively and all had too readily resorted to the mobilization of arms.

From the discussion, it was gleaned that in Nairobi the person on the street was generally supportive of President Hussein. But this sentiment was interpreted as support for a courageous third world underdog in confrontation with an assertive superpower. The allies were perceived as the big-power bullies and therefore not favored, in the same way that the International Monetary Fund and the World Bank are not favored by an extraordinarily sensitive African public.

It was reported that, far from inciting divisions between Muslims and Christians in Africa, the Gulf War had the effect of bringing them together. Non-Westerners were suffering at the hands of Western bullies, providing reason sufficient for Muslims and Christians in Africa to espouse common views and generate common opinions.

There was a query as to why anyone would expect churches in Africa to be more exercised about the Gulf War than they were about the continuing wars in Africa: in Ethiopia, Somalia, Liberia, Mozambique, Angola, and Mauritania-Senegal. Several of these wars had been addressed by African church leaders with varying degrees of intensity and with mixed results. Generally, action by African churches had been specific to the war at hand. Except for the continued pronouncements on South Africa, churches had not articulated common positions on Africa's wars; nor had war, per se, been addressed either as a theological or as a continental issue.

This discussion was informed by two ends of a spectrum: on the one hand, there was a felt need to side with the "underdog," as God is in solidarity with the poor and the weak. On the other hand, there was the view that love must prevail and not become unduly preoccupied with the details and demands of complex politics. A middle position held that no conflict should be left to its own dynamics and devices. The church always has the duty to offer alternatives, to identify common ground between antagonists, to suggest entry points toward resolution of conflict, and to stand by in support as alternatives to armed conflict are tested.

A question was raised about any real or apparent similarities between the invasion of Kuwait and border conflicts in Africa. Among others, the Tanzania-Uganda, Mauritania-Senegal, Kenya-Sudan, Kenya-Somalia, and Kenya-Uganda border skirmishes were cited. Churches in Africa were not known to have produced any serious comment on those situations.

There was a suggestion, finally, that the African public needed some guidance in thinking about the current Gulf War. Questions regarding the apportioning of blame, the Christian/Muslim factors, the third world/first world factors, and the long-term/short-term purposes of the war all need to be identified and located within some articulated perspective. At the time of this meeting, such reflection was being done reasonably well by some of the Nairobi newspapers, though official biases showed. Could or should the church offer more disinterested guidance? The question remained an open challenge.

General Observations

In African newspapers, a variety of perspectives were on offer: there was sophisticated analysis and there was cynicism. For some reporters, this was a war of the powerful being meted out at the expense of the weak: simply another manifestation of crude, insensitive power being exercised. While direct and immediate consequences for Africa (such as higher fuel prices, higher import/export costs, collapsing tourist trade, dramatic cuts in airline operations, and so on) as a result of the fighting were anticipated, in general it was a war "out there," overshadowed by the half dozen ongoing civil wars in as many African countries. Both the Gulf War and African wars were perceived by this small group to be "managed" by northern/Western media agencies. It happened only that the Gulf War via the CNN system was reflected in vastly greater detail and with greater intensity than were the ongoing wars in Africa. Why should any of these wars be singled out for special concern? All of them were perceived, in some measure, as taking place at Africa's expense; all were debilitating and all would be subjected eventually to the phenomenon of "concern fatigue."

The Position of African Governments

On the question of the Gulf War, African governments were not united. Senegal, Sierra Leone, and Niger actually committed combatants in support of the Western Allied forces. On the other hand, Algeria, Zambia, and Ghana made efforts to mediate between the protagonists, once the war had begun. Some countries with strong Muslim populations expressed popular support for Iraq but official support for the allies. Others voiced criticism addressed to all protagonists, but did so cautiously. After all, many African countries enjoyed access to Western largesse and were not keen to jeopardize existing relationships, however uncomfortable and fragile those relationships were deemed to be.

The Root Causes of the War

Such queries posed more elements than could be readily analyzed. Opinions ranged as broadly as the range of sophistication in Africa. Newspapers carried in-depth commentary on the root causes, providing evidence that, at the analytic level, there was much understanding. In general, the range of opinion on this question was at least as diverse and complex in Africa as it was in Europe and the United States, but then in Africa there is the ever-present sense of being on the underside of the world's power configurations.

Agenda for the Future

Surely all people and agencies of goodwill would deplore the just-concluded Gulf War hostilities. There was hope that an acceptable peace for the Middle East would be forged. But to identify aggressor or victim at that still-delicate moment would have proven a specious exercise. In every war, everyone loses to some extent. Had the time come to decry all war as an instrument of public and international policy? Could partners in North Atlantic countries join churches in Africa for a serious review of "just war" theology? Could the findings of the WCC's Justice, Peace and Integrity of Creation theme be finessed into an inclusive theology, in support of all life? Was it reasonable to expect all churches and church-related agencies to pronounce in favor of life—*all* life—and against all violent death?

The need for reflection on the meaning of the Gulf War was not easily ignored. Even after the cessation of armed hostilities, the extent of the destruction and disruption was only beginning to make an impression. Preliminary evidence suggested that Iraq was severely damaged economically and destabilized politically. The Soviet Union as an erstwhile ally of Iraq was forced to reassess the whole of its military support. Various personalities and political factions within the Arab world now needed to reexamine prospects for the future while the specter of continued foreign military presence in the region loomed. In the meantime, the dead were being counted and buried.

During recent decades, Africa has shifted from a preoccupation with wars of liberation to civil wars, from the euphoria of political independence to understandings of the stresses and strains of nation building and to the management of modern state apparatus. Churches had reflected the changing moods. Typical was a statement from the churches in Liberia: "Within the last few years, and especially in 1990, the Church has witnessed an increase in violence that has resulted in the killing and uprooting of persons, destruction of properties, the forced separation of families and the lack of proper and correct information to the public. The Church is concerned about the recent killings, harassment and intimidation of persons in Monrovia. These ugly, unchristian, uncivilized and barbaric acts have claimed our attention as servants of God. It is to this end that we, the Christian population of Liberia, express our strong condemnation and disapproval of violence" (May 30, 1990).

This statement expressed the agony of violence in the present time. Peace initiatives taken by churches in Africa could be cited—the list is now impressive. Indeed, mediation and conciliation activity may well have outpaced theological reflection on war and violence. The Gulf War and the continuing African wars served as reminders of unfinished agenda.

—Mid-1990s, Nairobi, Kenya

16
Joint Theological Conference: Observations and Comments

Introduction

With special permission from the organizers, I was able to attend this conference as an observer. I was one of two expatriate "missionary" types in attendance; the other was Briton John Padwick, long time Church Missionary Society associate working with the Organization of African Instituted Churches (OAIC). What follows is a reflection on the comments and deliberations of the meeting as filtered through my personal observations (and biases). Together with five other participants of the meeting, I was involved with the process of formulating the final communiqué.

It had been apparent for some time that theological debates on issues of the day served as important reference points to the change process underway in Africa. These discussions functioned in that very significant space/distance between what was perceived to have been "delivered" by the Western missionary enterprise, on the one hand, and what had been received, on the other, by the Christian believer community in Africa. An observer in this meeting could easily have gotten the initial impression that this space was fraught; many of the presenters spoke of chaotic disarray in the arena of religious belief and praxis in Africa. However, both the deliberations and the conclusions of the conference gave evidence, ultimately, of working on a positive creative edge of this transition time. According to Prof. Douglas Waruta, one of the organizers of the conference, this meeting provided a continental forum where the ongoing conversation regarding Africa's reception and practice of the Gospel intersected with a critical examination of the continent's multi-pronged religio-cultural heritage.

Participants at this conference generally identified themselves as members of the Protestant ecumenical community, representing the interests and concerns of the "mainline churches," also referred to repeatedly as the "historic missionary-instituted" churches in Africa. For this community of churches, the All Africa Conference of Churches (AACC) served as the continental umbrella organization. In this meeting the OAIC, with its fascinating and complex history, was "welcomed into the mainline fold." They had distinguished themselves by separating from the historic mission churches and by claiming to reflect more authentically African expressions of Christianity. The contested issues related to perceived discrimination, to foreign cultural impositions, and, generally, to a Gospel too much overlaid by Western cultural accruements. In recent decades, the AICs had been researched and courted by the ecumenical community even as many of the AICs had variously sought and achieved a measure of "mainline acceptance" by affiliating with National Christian Councils, the AACC, and the World Council of Churches (WCC).

Each of the respective groups attending this conference had explored and developed its distinctive theological concerns. For example, as indicated in the communiqué, the Circle of Concerned African Women Theologians (aka the Circle) comprised female theologians in Africa and their unique concerns. Organizers of the conference had gone to great lengths to invite Catholic and evangelical theologians, but none of them responded to the invitation. Theologians from the more recently arrived charismatic (healing, crusades, wealth) missionary communities were viewed, and viewed themselves, as even more distanced from the concerns of mainline theologians. People who still maintained loyalties to the East African Revival tradition would generally not have been comfortable with the theologizing being pursued by this conference. Thus, as a preliminary observation, much of the very wide spectrum of theological reflection in Africa remained outside the purview of this meeting despite its ecumenical, inclusive claims.

Comments/Observations

Keynote

Musindi Kanyori, a Kenyan theologian, presented the keynote address. She set a striking, strident tone, beginning with and apologizing for her litany of lamentations: AIDS, poverty, social violence, child soldiers ("our children are killing us"), among much else. But she also posed the questions: How is it that Africans survive? What kind of strength is on display ("People seem to be living as if freedom and hope do exist")?

We must "worry with God" about the meaning of creation; God's wisdom is never individual wisdom. God's wisdom is exercised in community; it is the wisdom which emerges in the "reclaiming of dialogue" among all elements of society, including, in particular, the grassroots of society. From the biblical perspective, the central questions always being addressed by Christians are: "Who do people say that I am?" "Who do you say that I am?"

Grand Narratives

Within AACC circles, the paradigm of reconstruction had been widely explored, especially since the end of the Cold War. That demise seemed to provide a sharp break in Africa's sojourn, spurring the quest for a shift from the paradigm of liberation, which had informed African theological reflection since the 1960s and earlier. In this conference, the paradigm of reconstruction was challenged; it was deemed inadequate to the complex situation on the continent, and it was considered unhelpful to rely on a single, overarching "grand narrative" to explain the dynamics underway. In any case, the paradigm of reconstruction had been too closely related to the demise of the Cold War, making it easy to forget the extraordinary protest dynamics of the 1950s and '60s, which still provided a basis for reflection and analysis. One participant cited the powerful discussions in the '60s around many strong writings—among others, Okot p'Bitek's *Song of Lawino*.

Furthermore, if reconstruction were accepted as the operative paradigm, what was being reconstructed, and according to whose pattern? Then current popular lament in Africa commonly focused on the breakdown of modern sector services, or conversely on the breakdown of religio-cultural mores, which were more characteristic of the "village" in Africa. Were the services and "efficiencies" of the colonial era to be reinstated, or should Africa now focus on other priorities? And if the passing of village mores is mourned, will they be revisited or ignored by design or default? If by design, by which criteria shall the rapidly fading values of the village be analyzed and selectively reaffirmed (*reconstructed*)? Women participants were especially adamant that much from the village must be abandoned and even condemned; on many counts, the ways of the African village had been unkind to the women of the continent. Today, it was further noted, some African commentators are more negative with regard to African culture than were the early missionaries.

Human Sexuality

"There is a woman in this assembly whose back bears the marks of severe beating by her husband!" This was but one of the startling statements made by Dr. Mercy Oduyoye, easily recognized as the doyenne of African women theologians. She shared with many African women theologians an understanding that both the biblical and the African cultural heritage seemed to have conspired to make life difficult for African women. The Circle of Concerned African Women Theologians provided one of the safe places where African women theologians could discuss and heal the wounds that the excesses of patriarchy—from a variety of sources—had visited upon them.

As a cultural pattern of marriage in Africa, polygamy was deemed to be slowly disappearing from the modern sector population, but certain of its values had yet to be expunged from prevailing attitudes. Witness what typically happened to the African widow upon the death of her husband: in many cases, in-laws made off with the property that the late husband and the remaining widow had jointly acquired. This widespread practice seemed to indicate that the woman continued to be viewed as property to be exploited and discarded with the dissolution of the marriage union. Even the merest suggestion that polygamy could be an option for the modern African woman received the strongest negative reaction from the women present in the meeting. Like many other issues, the place of women in the new Africa had yet to be clearly defined.

Globalization–Mission

At its worst, globalization was declared an example of a negative working paradigm for this planet. Even though it had not been fully defined, it was already recognized as the dominant dynamic of the present time. Global electronic media facilities are among the most powerful current manifestations of this dynamic. But for discerning theologians, globalization is of course not entirely new to this continent. To this day the imperial languages of English, French, and Portuguese dominate modern sub-Saharan discourse. (In the final communiqué these languages, plus Arabic, were recognized as necessary to modern global communication.)

The advent in Africa of the missionary religions of Islam and Christianity was cited as an element of the globalizing process. Missionary religions, it was deemed, had arrived in Africa, consciously and unconsciously, at the expense of indigenous religious expressions. One participant noted that the Western missiological penchant for the quantification of the growth of Christianity in Africa was perceived by some observers in Africa as an example of negative globalization. (The final communiqué did acknowledge with appreciation the growth of the church in Africa.) The archbishop of an African Instituted Church lamented that his church had suffered from excessive research by overseas academics and by elite African researchers to the extent that the self-identity of the church had lurched into jeopardy. In this context, Mercy Oduyoye posed hard questions: "Is Africa the mission field for all cultures [and religions]?" "What does Africa contribute to global culture?" According to her, too much of African "dancing" has been done in "borrowed cultural robes."

While most of the comments on globalization were negative or cautionary, some participants lauded the virtues of the internet and email. Indeed, most of the participants used email and thus were caught up in the clutches of the future even as the mores of the past and present were being sorted out. There was a strong sense that the technologies of the West are "done to" Africa; they are not chosen by Africans from a list of clear alternatives, to say nothing of the fact that Africa is not actively creating its own technologies.

African Ecumenism

In his formal presentation, the General Secretary of the AACC mentioned—without elaboration—the declining commitment on the part of the mainline churches to ecumenism. In subsequent discussion it was lamented that the symbols of ecumenism such as "alliance" (multidenominational or interdenominational) secondary schools and seminaries were either being disbanded or undermined by a fresh explosion of denominational seminaries and universities. In many instances this trend was perceived as acquiescence to the negative dynamics of ethnicity and chauvinist denominationalism.

In passing it could be noted that the ecumenical impulse of the mainline churches in Africa was held together for decades by the challenge of continental liberation. When South Africa finally achieved majority rule in 1994, African ecumenicity lost much of its raison d'être, even as the Organization of African Unity (sometimes cited as the political opposite number to the AACC) was obliged to redefine itself. Anti-apartheid sentiments had for decades serviced cohesive continental resolve to work for the demise of the final citadel of "colonial" (in this case, European minority) rule. Just as the Soviet Union had collapsed after the Cold War into separate independent republics—often along religio-ethnic fault lines—so did Africa's fissures became more evident after the demise of apartheid. The ecumenical community meanwhile had not been able to articulate a clear vision for the future. The ambivalence of this meeting concerning the paradigm of reconstruction or any other single narrative attested to the dilemma (parenthetically, the theme of the next AACC assembly would be "Arise and Build"). Among others, these would seem to be the reasons for the current lack of enthusiasm for African ecumenicity. In discussion, participants also noted that the institutional expression (National Christian Councils, etc.) of African ecumenicity had been too readily and too uncritically adopted from the missionary period. It was further observed that the ecumenical agenda was quickly subverted by the development agenda and the ready access to funds that were on offer during the "development decades" of the 1960s and '70s—so declared by the United Nations.

African Instituted Churches

As early as the 1940s, "independent" churches were recognized as significant religious phenomena in Africa. The late Bengt Sunkler (Swedish missionary and missiologist) broke new ground with his book *Bantu Prophets in South Africa*. Later there were successive attempts to bring order to this greatly diverse category of Christian expression functioning outside the parameters of the missionary-instituted churches. One of the enduring umbrella organizations for these churches is the Organization of African Instituted Churches, with its headquarters in Nairobi. In his careful explanations, the AIC archbishop presenter revisited the meticulous choice of the word "instituted." During their efforts to register the OAIC, the leaders of the movement discovered that the term "independent" was viewed askance by the government of Kenya; it was taken as an indication of rebellion and popular discontent, a designation that would not bode well in post-independent Africa. Hence the word "instituted" as part of the official designation for this category of churches. Today AICs constitute 20 percent of the Christian population in Kenya and approximately 50 percent in South Africa.

In terms of their origins and religious practice, AICs had identified early on with the protest against colonial regimes (in Kenya they identified with the Mau Mau movement): they had protested the grabbing of land by European settlers; they had insisted on instituting and managing their own schools; they had resisted the Western character of missionary Christianity; and they had sought a more culturally acceptable expression of African Christianity. As a community of churches, they were suspicious of Western-style development, but on the other hand they had been greatly concerned to strengthen community life at grassroot levels. Indeed, they perceived Western-style development as inimical to community life. As a consequence of their strong protest against colonial regimes, they found it difficult to be critical of Africa's independent governments when the latter became more oppressive during the 1970s, '80s, and '90s.

The participation of the OAIC in this meeting was viewed as significant. While the AICs had enjoyed much attention from mainline churches and all manner of researchers, they had not been completely successful in commending themselves to their mainline co-religionists, and latterly they had experienced a crisis of identity among themselves. What were now their reasons for existing separately from the mainline churches? Were their original founding protestations adequate to the requirements of the future? Their participation in this convocation of theologians was seen as a forum in which such questions could begin to be addressed and, as noted earlier, as a coming closer to the mainline family of churches.

Conclusions

Theologians are academicians. In this meeting, many of the theologians were also clergy and senior church personalities. Together, their final plea was for greater cohesion in the curricula of seminaries throughout the churches on the continent and in the departments of religious studies in the continent's many secular universities. This to the end of the greater glory of God and to the practice of a faith that is at once authentically Christian and authentically situated in Africa.

—*August 2000, Nairobi*

Joint Theological Conference AACC/Circle/CATI/EATWOT/OAIC (Summary Reflections)

August 14–17, 2000
Mbagathi, Nairobi

Theme: "The Church Making a Difference in the Twenty-First Century"

As participants of the theological community of the African church, we have come together from fifteen countries in Africa, from two countries of the African diaspora, and from one Asian country, to meet at Mbagathi, Nairobi, Kenya, from 14 to 15 August, 2000, to reflect on our calling and ministry. We have gathered as representatives of the All Africa Conference of Churches (AACC), the Circle of Concerned African Women Theologians, the Conference of African Theological Institutions (CATI), the Ecumenical Association of Third World Theologians (EATWOT), and the Organization of African Instituted Churches (OAIC). We acknowledge with thanks the financial assistance and facilitation of the World Council of Churches (WCC). We have prayed and studied the Bible together and listened to the stories of our people, and we have been profoundly challenged by the present crisis in our continent to clarify our role in the service of the church and the wider community.

Concerns and Recommendations for Action

The conference notes the following issues and concerns for reflection and action:

1. We lament over the African contest and the African crisis. We lament our moral decline, the religious disharmony, and the political conflicts on our continent; the debt burden and the impact of Structural Adjustment Programs; our dependency on foreign aid, the widespread practice of gender violence; corruption in our governments, in society, and in the church; and the ever-growing

pandemic of HIV/AIDS. We lament in the understanding that our lamentation drives us to a vision of justice and hope for the future of our continent.

2. In these circumstances, and in order to fully comprehend our situation, the church must be involved in dialogue and solidarity with people at the grassroots; with women, people with disabilities, and others at the margins; and with people of other religious persuasions, so that their concerns and voices become part of our theological reflection and our lives. We value in particular the contribution of AACC, the Circle, and EATWOT in this regard, and encourage them in their endeavors to promote an inclusive and relevant theology.

3. We affirm that the cornerstone of all our theological reflection must be the inviolability of the dignity and humanity of our African peoples. We reject racism, ethnocentrism, and other ideologies that divide our peoples. This affirmation should also form the basis of our collaboration and relationships with our partners in the North.

4. In order to realize the full potential of the church in Africa, we recognize the urgent need for our churches and theological institutions to take affirmative action in order to rectify the gender imbalance in our church ministries and in all decision-making processes, in the staffing and enrollment in our theological seminaries, and in the articulation and development of our theologies. In this context we recognize and value the role of women's organizations such as the Circle that create a safe space for women to articulate and develop their own concerns for the benefit of the whole church and community.

5. We note with approval the WCC's forthcoming Decade to Overcome Violence (2001–2010), and commit ourselves to work to identify the root causes of violence in our churches and societies, to conscientize our peoples, and to develop appropriate mechanisms and programs to deal with this menace. In our own context, we have identified violence against women and children, including domestic violence, female genital mutilation, ritual murders, and

witchcraft accusations as a special priority. We acknowledge and repent of the church's share in responsibility for all these forms of violence, both by commission and by omission.

6. Recognizing that the African situation is rapidly changing, diverse, and complex, we note the need to beware of trying to impose a grand narrative as the basis for our theological reflection. We therefore urge the AACC to recognize, encourage, and nurture the diverse theological models on our continent.

7. We urge the church in Africa to look for and mobilize local sources of finance for our theological and ecumenical institutions, and to develop strategies for their better management. We believe that self-reliance and self-financing are critical for African peoples' ownership of theological programs, of our institutions of learning, and of our church structures, theologies, and development. Self-reliance is also central to the development of personal dignity, self-worth, and a positive self-image.

8. We note and deplore the apparent decline of ecumenism in Africa, and the growth of large denominational institutions such as theological seminaries and universities. In the light of this, we urge the church in Africa to evaluate its understanding of the African and biblical roots of ecumenism, if the gains we have already made are not to slip away in the promotion of denominational and parochial interests.

9. In this context, we value the leadership of AACC and the work of CATI, and consider that CATI's role as a coordinating and accrediting body needs to be strengthened so that we can discover what is actually being taught in our theological institutions, how it is taught, and by whom, to ensure the relevance and inclusiveness of our curricula. We affirm the vital importance of continuing theological education for the laity as well as for the clergy. We urge the churches to provide sufficient resources for the promotion of lay training centers, and theological institutions offering ministerial training to form links with these centers.

10. In view of the ongoing conflicts in our continent, we urge the church in Africa to look afresh at its relationship with other faiths and other religious groups, in order to develop an appropriate ministry and to promote tolerance and mutual acceptance in a pluralist society.
11. We note the challenges posed by globalization to our peoples and societies, in particular by the debt crisis, and we affirm the need to identify appropriate criteria for assessing the positive and negative potential of globalization for our continent, so that we may be able both to confront its evil aspects and to harness its forces for positive human development.
12. In the context of globalization, we affirm the importance of encouraging mother tongues, such as in Bible translations. However, in order that Africans may be able to speak to Africans, we also encourage multilingual competency in the four official languages of the continent (Arabic, English, French, and Portuguese) as a means of communication between ourselves. In addition, we encourage the churches of Africa to develop local theologies, christologies, pneumatologies, and ecclesiologies. The promotion of such local identities is an essential response to the impact of globalization.
13. We commit ourselves to developing hermeneutical principles that will enable us to clarify the interface between our theological concerns of gospel and culture, gender, race, sexuality, and other faiths.
14. We acknowledge both the reader-centered approach and the historical-critical approach as effective instruments for the practice of biblical hermeneutics. These approaches enable our theological students to learn how to theologize as a way of life and can motivate them to participate in social transformation, rather than simply concentrating on the reception and transmission of content. We recognize the special contribution of EATWOT and the Circle in this regard.
15. In order to build the church for today and for the future, we recognize the essential need to acknowledge and value the visions and

dreams of our young people, and to enable them to share in the decision-making processes of our churches in order to realize their visions. Our churches should encourage our young people to value life and respect family and community values, through programs of Bible study, counseling, and guidance.

16. We recognize the participation of OAIC as the representative of the African Instituted Churches (AICs) at this conference as a sign that the AICs are slowly but surely moving from the margins to the center of the African church. As AICs and the so-called "historic" churches of Africa continue to learn from each other, the African church will move toward greater unity. As part of this process, we urge the full recognition of AICs and the new charismatic and Pentecostal churches as members of the body of Christ, and encourage their full involvement in ecumenical theological education and in pulpit exchanges with the so-called historic churches. We are, however, deeply concerned at the introduction of theologies—such as the so-called prosperity gospel—that exploit rather than liberate people, and that seek to enrich church ministers at the expense of their church members.

17. We recognize that both AICs and the new charismatic churches have a strong ministry of the Holy Spirit, a ministry that speaks to our peoples' spiritual needs and the African understanding of the spiritual world. The conference affirms the importance of revisiting the mission of the church—preaching, teaching, and healing—and urges our churches to examine, evaluate, and develop this ministry for the benefit of all the people of Africa. We also urge the churches of Africa to vigorously pursue policies and programs aimed at eradicating poverty in all its forms.

18. We note with concern the scarcity of theological works published in Africa, by Africans, for Africans. We therefore urge all our participating organizations to concert their efforts to publish and make available contemporary African theological texts.

19. We have benefited greatly from the participation at this conference by members of the African diaspora and from other Third World

countries. We affirm that Africa is wider than the continent itself, and we seek the liberation of all the sons and daughters of Africa across the world. We therefore commit ourselves to strengthening the solidarity and links between the mother continent and members of the diaspora, especially through student and staff exchanges. In this connection, we value the ongoing MacAdd initiative of the WCC and the AACC.

20. We urge the churches to tackle vigorously the root causes of HIV/AIDS. This requires among other things an honesty and openness on issues of human sexuality that has hitherto been lacking among our churches and people, and a commitment to Christian education for behavioral change. We deplore the actions of some churches that actually hinder the process of education and prevention.

21. Land is the source of life for the great majority of the people of Africa. We encourage the churches to look critically at the issue of land owned by the few and denied to the many, and to propose appropriate action in the light of gospel values so that all the people of our continent may enjoy justice, peace, and prosperity.

22. We look to the future and are committed to dialogue on these issues. This in itself is a sign of hope for our continent. We rejoice at the numerical growth of the church in Africa, at the emergence of grassroots theologies, and at the great resilience of its suffering peoples. We celebrate with them the presence of the kingdom of God among us and commit ourselves, under God and in the power of the Holy Spirit, to work for the spread of the good news of Jesus Christ, and the fuller realization of the kingdom of God in the lives of all our people.

17
Publications Supported by MCC

Introduction

Mennonite Central Committee in East Africa supported the publication of a number of books. There was never anything like a strategic plan guiding the way toward support for publishing ventures. However, one can detect something like an intuitive DNA that was somehow tripped into action while I was on assignment in Tanzania during the mid-1960s. I had been seconded by Eastern Mennonite Board of Missions to the Christian Council of Tanzania as secretary for relief and service. This assignment, together with the general "buzz," offered a front-row seat to many pivotal issues of the day. Quite unwittingly, we had been plopped into one of the most creative cauldrons on the African continent.

Dar es Salaam, the capital of Tanzania, was host at the time to a great variety of liberation movements from all over Africa, representing peoples still under colonial or apartheid rule. We heard about leaders from Rhodesia (now Zimbabwe), Mozambique, South West Africa (now Namibia), Guinea-Bissau, and Angola, jostling for position, power, and independence.

Meanwhile, Julius Nyerere, the president of Tanzania, was in the process of articulating his philosophy of "African Socialism," locally known as "Ujamaa" (familyhood)—a sociopolitical formulation at variance with the dyed-in-the-wool Marxist socialism of the day.

For many idealistic youth from the Western world, inspired in part by the push of US president John F. Kennedy's talk about a "frontier" ethos and in part by the pull of President Nyerere's philosophizing and experiment in nation-building, Tanzania had become something of a magnet.

With strong guidance from the World Council of Churches, the respective national councils of churches in Africa were offering guidance for the transition from missionary to African leadership, a phenomenon taking place primarily within Africa's mainline Protestant churches.

There was a widespread understanding that the national Christian councils in Africa—direct heirs to the mainline Protestant missionary fellowships that had long facilitated coordination on education and medical services as well as Bible translation and distribution—also functioned as conduits for the transition from colonial rule to independent governance structures controlled by Africans.

This auxiliary political role of the Christian councils in Africa can be traced to the fact that many of Africa's emerging nationalist, liberationist politicians of the day had been educated in missionary or church-sponsored schools. All of these elements were present and variously accessible from within the Christian Council of Tanzania.

But in retrospect, additional factors provided a strong learning context. For example, Ezram Mariogo, a young Mennonite graduate from a secondary school in northwest Tanzania, had just arrived in Dar es Salaam from study in the US, sporting a recently acquired master's degree and a bride from the Caribbean. As a latent or budding nationalist, he pointed us to the book *Muntu* by Janheinz Jahn, which set out a remarkably clear and positive overview of African culture and religion.

Later, we became acquainted with *Bantu Philosophy* (1945) by Placid Tempels, a Catholic Belgian missionary in the Congo, and *The Phenomenon of Man* (1956) by Teilhard de Chardin, the Jesuit paleontologist. We learned that presidents Nyerere of Tanzania, Kaunda of Zambia, and Senghor of Senegal were reading the Chardin book at the time. Someone (possibly Nyerere) was said to have mused: "How is it possible that a European can think thoughts so profound and so similar to African thoughts?"

And then there was the world of music. In Dar es Salaam, Annetta quickly became aware of the wealth of Tanzania's folk song tradition. Her interest in this area had been piqued by our 1964 visit to Hungary, where the noted ethnomusicologist Zoltán Kodály had developed a sophisticated music education pedagogy based on the country's indigenous folk song tradition. (Years later, Annetta acquired the equivalent of a master's degree at the Kodály Institute of the Franz Liszt Academy of Music in Hungary.) Together with a creative music teacher colleague in the Dar es Salaam Music Conservatoire, Annetta became engaged in a countrywide process, seeking to incorporate the Tanzanian folk song tradition into the country's modern music pedagogy.

At the time, significant aspects of the missionary posture in Africa were still dominated by condescending views toward African culture and religion, as well as the emerging language of "development." These elements portrayed Africa as a place of need and deprivation, ready for redefinition and solutions offered by armies of advisors and development workers from the North Atlantic world.

Against these odds, it slowly became clear that we were witnessing a serious contest between Africa's self-definition and its search for a place in the world, on the one hand, and Western analyses and definitions of Africa within the modern world, on the other. Consciously and unconsciously, we became aware that Africa's self-understanding was the most credible one in this contest; clearly Africa was serving as its own best resource. All of our assignments subsequent to the Dar es Salaam experience only reinforced those initial impressions.

The publications noted below were all, in one way or other, supported by MCC. Some of them reached the publication stage with only monetary support from MCC. Others required much actual writing time and extensive engagement with African authors. Several of the manuscripts had to be pursued and the authors persuaded that publication was a desirable goal. Some required only facilitation with empathetic publishers. All of these publications provided occasions to meet interesting people and to become involved with fascinating processes. We are grateful for this incredibly rich experience.

50 Kenyan Folk Songs to Sing and Play
Annetta Miller
Kenya Conservatoire of Music
Nairobi, Kenya, 1984

A collection of fifty songs from around Kenya, arranged in order of increasing complexity, and intended as elementary-school classroom resource.

A Pocket Directory of Trees and Seeds in Kenya
Wayne Teel
KENGO
Nairobi, Kenya, 1984

This book was compiled to answer two basic tree-planting questions for Kenyans: Which trees are the best to plant in a particular climate type? And where does one obtain the requisite seeds or seedlings? Ninety tree species are described. For each tree species, a list of possible seed sources is provided. The book was illustrated by Terry Hirst, whose daughter Wanjira (Ciira) later married our son Edward.

Anecdote by Wayne Teel

My favorite story related to the book concerns a fellow from the border area of Kisii and South Nyanza District in western Kenya. He was a small farmer who grew coffee. As I remember, he had between three and four hundred trees. He got a copy of the book from one of the Peace Corps fellows working with the Ministry of Energy projects in Kisii under Amare Getahun. He came to Nairobi and sought me out. He was intrigued about growing trees between his coffee plants, and wanted me to come and see his farm. So I went. Turned out he had already planted trees in between his coffee. He recognized the names of a bunch of local trees in the book because we had put the local names prominently under the botanical names. From that, he figured he could not lose by planting those trees, so he went ahead and grew some from seed. They included *Erythrina abyssinica*, *Markhamia lutea* (formerly *platycalyx*), and *Sesbania sesban*. That was about the quickest turnaround time for planting of trees that I remember.

Introducing the Camel: Basic Camel Keeping for the Beginner
Peter Grill
United Nations Environment Programme: Desertification Control
Programme Activity Center
Nairobi, Kenya, 1986

Increasing droughts and desertification placed a severe burden on Kenya. Camel husbandry was perceived by many government and development strategists to be a viable means of reducing the effects of drought and desertification. This handbook was intended to provide a concise yet basic resource on camel husbandry in Kenya, for the benefit of livestock technicians, development agents, and field workers.

The State of Seed in Kenya
Kamoji Wachira
KENGO
Nairobi, Kenya, 1986

This booklet represented an attempt to highlight the precarious legal and genetic situation in Kenya with regard to the country's facility to collect, preserve, enhance, and propagate the seeds of essential food crops. When he researched and wrote this text, Kamoji Wachira had just been released from prison. His incarceration had been occasioned by an association with intellectuals who were protesting what was deemed to be oppressive rule of the Kenya government. Before his imprisonment, he was a lecturer in the biology department of Kenyatta University College. Later he moved to Canada, where he has enjoyed an illustrious career as a development consultant with the Canadian International Development Agency.

Let's Learn Music: Introducing Musical Skills—A Sequential Approach to Music Education
Annetta Miller
International Publishing Services/Baptist Publications House
Nairobi, Kenya, 1987

Let's Learn Music was intended as a bridge between African oral music and the beginnings of Western music notation. Annetta drew from a vast number of folk songs and presented simple notated musical elements in an understandable fashion. The book uses African folk songs as building blocks for written musical forms.

The Gene Hunters: Biotechnology and the Scramble for Seeds
Calestous Juma
Princeton University Press
Princeton, New Jersey, 1989

Financial support for the publication of this book was provided jointly by Lutheran World Relief and the Mennonite Central Committee. It was published originally by Zed Press in Britain and later by Princeton University Press in the US. This book is still in print and is recognized as a classic study of issues with worldwide relevance. Calestous Juma went on to become Professor of the Practice of International Development at Harvard University.

Luo Spirituals: African Choral Works
Samuel Otieno
Africa Center for Technology Studies
Nairobi, Kenya, 1990

Annetta Miller assisted with the editing and preparation of this edition assembled by Samuel Otieno, a Kenyan musician.

Origen the Egyptian: A Literary and Historical Consideration of the Egyptian Background in Origen's Writings on Martyrdom
Nancy Heisey
Paulines Publications Africa
Nairobi, Kenya, 2000

Origen, the third-century theologian and biblical scholar, has often been described as one of the great representatives of Alexandrian Christian theology. Scholars have debated whether he was truly a man of the church or a philosopher imbued with Greek concepts and ideals. Few have seriously considered the role played by his heritage as an Egyptian. This study probes Origen's writings on martyrdom, an issue of serious import for Christians of his time.

Nancy Heisey worked for MCC in the Congo and Burkina Faso. She later became Professor of Biblical Studies and Church History at Eastern Mennonite University, and served as president of the Mennonite World Conference.

Anecdote from Nancy Heisey

I think my favorite connection was when Laurenti Magesa visited us in 2003. Paul and I had him for dinner and we got to talking about his book *African Religion: Moral Traditions for Abundant Life* and my Origen book. He was so interested—in fact, he was the person most interested in my book, other than Calvin Shenk. So we exchanged autographed copies. When I looked later at the note he had written in my copy of his book, it read "African Renaissance." I took this as a gesture of inclusion in that hopeful undertaking.

Dinka Christianity: The Origins and Development of Christianity among the Dinka of Sudan with Special Reference to the Songs of Dinka Christians
(Faith in Sudan Series No. 11)
Marc R. Nikkel
Paulines Publications Africa
Nairobi, Kenya, 2001

Marc Nikkel undertook pioneering work in collaboration with Nathaniel Garang, Episcopal bishop of Bor, in developing short local training programs. This work gave him opportunity to reflect upon the continuing revolution in Dinka spiritual perspectives and allegiance.

Suffering and God: A Theological Reflection on the War in Sudan
(Faith in Sudan Series No. 13)
Isaiah Dau
Paulines Publications Africa
Nairobi, Kenya, 2002

Isaiah Dau is a senior pastor of the Sudan Pentecostal Churches and is currently principal of a Pentecostal Bible School in Kenya, sponsored by the Pentecostal Evangelistic Fellowship of Kenya. He lived through some of the most searing periods of the war and describes how his life has been profoundly affected. This work may be the first substantial theological reflection by a Sudanese on the theological meaning of the war and the suffering it has engendered.

Isaiah Dau's career in Christian ministry was launched under the tutelage of Anglican Bishop Nathaniel Garang of South Sudan. Later, Dau was affiliated with the Pentecostal Church. Financial support for his doctoral studies was provided by Tear Fund, a British evangelical agency. His doctoral studies were supervised by a white South African in a South African university. The publication of his book was funded by Mennonite Central Committee and published by Paulines Publications Africa—a Catholic agency. All in all, an unusual ecumenical project!

Sharing Boundaries: Learning the Wisdom of Africa
Annetta Miller
Paulines Publications Africa
Nairobi, Kenya, 2003
Published in German as *Begegnungen und Fremdheit: Von der Weisheit Afrikas Lernen*, translated by Anton Schneider, 2005

This book contains fifty vignettes, presented in free-verse format, on a variety of African life themes.

Southern Sudan: Too Many Agreements Dishonoured
Abel Alier
Paulines Publications Africa
(originally published by Ithaca Press in 1990)
Nairobi, Kenya, 2003

This is a reprint of the original 1990 Ithaca Press publication. Mennonite Central Committee representatives to Sudan (1999–2005) were approached by the executive secretary of the New Sudan Council of Churches, Rev. Haruun Ruun, to assist in the production of this republication. In the event, the reprinted edition became available, strategically, during the height of the two-year negotiation process in Naivasha, Kenya, between the government of Sudan and the Sudan People's Liberation Movement. The agreement that emerged from these protracted negotiations is known as the Comprehensive Peace Agreement (CPA). In a public ceremony on January 9, 2005, in Nairobi, the protagonists finally signed the CPA document. During a prolonged introductory speech, the late Col. John Garang, founder and leader of the Sudan People's Movement, lifted high a copy of this book, noting its importance to the negotiated peace process.

The Kalenjiin People's Egypt Origin Legend Revisited: Was Isis Asiis?
Kipkoeech araap Sambu
Longhorn Publishers
Nairobi, Kenya, 2007

In this book, the author reexamines the ancient Egyptian divine figures, such as Isis and Ptah, and draws connections with Kalenjin traditions. He similarly revisits various other ancient Egyptian deity figures, such as *Maat*, whose names and theological essences have connections with the Kalenjin language, nomenclature, and religion.

Dr. Sambu's book became a best-seller in Kenya. With income from this book, Sambu produced a second book entitled *The Misiri Legend Explored: A Linguistic Inquiry into the Kalenjiin People's Oral Tradition of Ancient Egyptian Origin*, published by the Nairobi University Press.

African Wisdom Calendars
Annetta Miller

The following six desk flip-calendars feature an African proverb for each day of the year on the respective themes. These proverbs, gleaned over a period of several decades, form part of Annetta Miller's vast proverb collection, numbering well over a hundred thousand. In Africa, the calendars have been distributed through the continental sales network of Paulines Publications Africa, and in the United States and Canada through the sales network of Ten Thousand Villages. The calendars on water and trees were sponsored and distributed, respectively, by Sahelian Solutions (SASOL) and Excellent Development (Kenya).

African Wisdom on War and Peace
Annetta Miller
Paulines Publications Africa
Nairobi, Kenya, 2004

African Wisdom for Life
Annetta Miller
Paulines Publications Africa
Nairobi, Kenya, 2005

African Wisdom on Leadership
Annetta Miller
Paulines Publications Africa
Nairobi, Kenya, 2006

African Wisdom on Water
Annetta Miller
SASOL Foundation
Kitui, Kenya, 2006

African Wisdom on Trees
Annetta Miller
Excellent Development (Kenya)
Machakos, Kenya, 2007

African Wisdom on the Sacred
Annetta Miller
Paulines Publications Africa
Nairobi, Kenya, 2009

The Murang'a Murals
Edited by Harold Miller
Nairobi, Kenya, 2009

The Murang'a murals are five spectacular floor-to-ceiling life-of-Christ paintings created by Tanzanian artist Elimo Njau during the mid-1950s on the north wall of the St. James and All Martyrs Cathedral in Murang'a, Kenya. This book includes articles on the murals and images of the murals themselves.

African Ethics: Gĩkũyũ Traditional Morality
Hannah Kinoti
Rodopi Press
Amsterdam, Netherlands, 2010
and Catholic University of Eastern Africa
Nairobi, Kenya, 2013

In extensive collaboration with family members of the late Dr. Hannah Kinoti, MCC funded a careful editing of her PhD dissertation on Kikuyu ethics. The book was subsequently published in the Netherlands. Funds for the publication of this book came from other sources.

18
Discerning the Times: Africa's Quest for a Future

THERE IS, according to the wise man of the Bible, "a time for everything"; "there is nothing new under the sun." Much has transpired since those words were written. In a shrinking global village, all are exposed to diverse perceptions of time; different peoples experience time differently. Discerning the times, then, has something to do with understanding the respective culture-bound temporal perceptions. Hence, this brief reflection.

One of Kenya's best-known theologians, John Mbiti, wrote in the 1960s on African perceptions of time. It was his contention—a contention not shared by all other African scholars, but interesting nonetheless—that time in Africa could be understood under two major categories: *zamani* ("past") and *sasa* ("present"). In this scheme of understanding, time flows from the present into the past. *Zamani* becomes the final storehouse of all phenomena and events, which slowly coalesce into an overarching reality.

Sasa, on the other hand, comprises the period of conscious living; it binds together individuals and their immediate experiential environment. The category of *sasa* can be subdivided into *potential* time and *actual* time. Potential time has to do with the predictable routines of the world, such as the rising and setting of the sun. Actual time, by contrast, refers to the composition of events taking place at any material time, and generally to events willed or initiated by people or events immediately affecting the awareness of people. In other words, actual time is a function of the human community interacting with events, whether willed by that community or taking the form of nonroutine acts of God. Logically, "what has not taken place or what has no likelihood of an immediate occurrence falls under the category of no time."

Mbiti's understanding of the future was considered controversial and intriguing. He claimed that African cosmologies and African languages do not reach into or touch the distant future. As a consequence, the future exerts less influence on everyday life than does *zamani*, and certainly less than does *sasa*. Thus, according to him, the discovery and extension of future time holds great potential for the shaping of the composite life of African peoples.

In applying Mbiti's time scheme to recent decades, one could think of *zamani* as the traditional past of Africa, when age was revered and wisdom lodged in the accumulated experience of the elders. If Africa's *sasa* were seen to comprise the decades immediately prior to and immediately following the independence period of the 1960s, then the reference was to a strong sense of dynamic awareness. Among African theologians, this time has been referred to as *exile* (colonial subservience), moving toward the *promised land* (political and spiritual independence). At the time of this writing, Africa's last colony, Namibia, had just gained independence and South Africa was undergoing major changes, shifting from minority toward majority rule. Kenyan theologian Jesse Mugambi asserted that the time of exile had already passed. Mugambi claimed that Africa was approaching the time of restoration, when gains would be consolidated, when identities would be reaffirmed, and when everyone would share in building beyond the *sasa*.

Africa's sense of *sasa* has been profoundly influenced by the north Atlantic world. Indeed, the effect of changes in eastern Europe after the demise of the Soviet Union and the creation of the European Community (1992) in western Europe had given rise in some African circles to fears of abandonment. Members of the ecumenical community in both Europe and Africa echoed similar sentiments. But according to some African academics, the future could be taken in hand; it could be anticipated and it could be created.

In 1987, a group of eminent African scholars met in Kericho, Kenya, to consider prospects for the future. They were committed to thinking beyond the widespread image of Africa as the continent of famines and poverty. For purposes of their reflection, they chose the one-hundred-year time frame from 1957—the year in which Ghana became independent—to 2057. According to their prognosis, over the following twenty to thirty years, there would be continuing decline in many sectors of African life. But hope was on the horizon. In particular, there was hope if decision makers and African collectivities (such as churches) committed themselves to the prospect of what the academics called "surprise-rich futures"—hopeful possibilities based on careful planning and concerted action.

The American Lutheran theologian Walter Brueggeman once asserted: "The future belongs to those with the language to possess it." He invoked the creative notion of "*languaging* our way" into desired or preferred futures. Imagining futures was not to be equated with "playing God"; neither was it intended as temporal sleight-of-hand nor as a quest for a mindless panacea. Rather, it called for strong visions, careful discernment within community, and faith mobilized into action. It required little genius or prophetic insight to denounce bad times. And these were deemed bad times.

By contrast, the mobilization toward hopeful futures was deemed to require the best of spiritual and community resources. It was precisely such resources to which the church in Africa laid claim. According to the wise man of the Bible, "there is a time for everything." Now is the time to work for God's future, for anticipating our common future. A profound *zamani* and an overwhelming *sasa* may, with due consideration, coalesce into a "surprise-rich" future for all.

—Mid-1990s, Nairobi, Kenya

About the Author

Harold Miller was born in Canton, Ohio, in 1935. He was nurtured to Christian faith within an Amish and Conservative Mennonite church community near Hartville, Ohio. From 1955 to 1958 he served in Germany as "PAX boy" in a program sponsored by the Mennonite Central Committee (MCC), building houses for European Mennonite refugees. He graduated from Eastern Mennonite College in Harrisonburg, Virginia, with a BA in History, and later earned an MA in International Affairs at Pittsburgh University.

After teaching history and civics at Eastern Mennonite High School in Harrisonburg, Virginia, from 1963 to 1965, he was seconded by Eastern Mennonite Board of Missions (EMM) to the Christian Council of Tanzania in Dar es Salaam, Tanzania, to the position of Secretary for Relief and Service from 1965 to 1971. For most of the period between 1972 and 1974 he was seconded by EMM in collaboration with MCC to the Sudan Council of Churches with its base in Khartoum, Sudan, as logistics officer. From 1974 to 1981 he was seconded to the National Council of Churches of Kenya based in Nairobi, Kenya, to the position of Secretary for Rural Development. From 1981 to 1987 he served as MCC's East Africa representative, providing administrative oversight for variously placed North American volunteers and workers, and for program initiatives that included a brief entitled "Food and Peace." From 1987 to 1989 he was appointed by MCC as co-administrator of the Horn of Africa Project, an initiative ensconced within Conrad Grebel College in Kitchener-Waterloo, Ontario. From 1989 to 1999 he was seconded by MCC to the All Africa Conference of Churches based in Nairobi, Kenya, to the position of consultant in its Department of International Affairs. From 1999 to 2005 he served as MCC's co-representative (together with his wife, Annetta) to Sudan, based in Nairobi, Kenya. Between 2005 and 2018, he and Annetta lived as retirees in Nairobi, Kenya. They currently reside in Harrisonburg, Virginia, and visit Kenya annually.

www.ingramcontent.com/pod-product-compliance
Lightning Source LLC
Chambersburg PA
CBHW031441040426
42444CB00007B/924